"Andrew has consistently delivered innovative research and insightful observations at a very high level. The Bionic Advisor is a timely snapshot of how AI and machine learning can be implemented in a new era for the best of breed global advisor. The detailed quantitative framework combined with his brilliant, insightful and pragmatic qualitative interpretation is easy to digest and very timely. This will quickly become the default reference for all advisors going forward."

GEORGE BOUBOURAS

Managing Director (MD), Research, Investments & Advisory, K2 Asset Management

"Andrew MacDonald has nailed it. The Bionic Adviser is a must-read for any individual or firm involved in providing Advice to its clients. The advent of AI is not another fad. Its impacts are far reaching and already being felt. My favourite quote in the book: "The real question isn't whether AI can replace what we do. It's whether we, as advisers, can evolve fast enough to stay relevant when our clients realise what's possible without our direct involvement. AI is not going away, learn where your real value is and use AI to magnify it. Experiment with it, integrate it and work with it. Early adopters won't look back."

KIERAN FORDE

Head of Adviser Channel – Zurich Financial Services Australia

"This is the book we've all been waiting for. At a time when confusion & fear often dominate the conversation about AI, The Bionic Advisor offers a clear and inspiring way forward. More than just a survival guide, it's a playbook for thriving, showing how the true future of advisory lies in harnessing the collective wisdom of humans and AI together. Andrew MacDonald charts a path that is both practical and visionary, helping us move beyond the hype to shape the future of the bionic advisor with confidence and optimism."

SAM FERNANDO

Learning & Leadership Leader, Aurecon

"The Bionic Advisor is a wake-up call. As ever with Andrew's message it is based on considered research, deep insight and incisive identification of solutions conveyed in a clear, committed style. Written with urgency, this tells us what we need to appreciate as we deal with the next revolution as advisors. Much like his World Class Advisor programme there is a practical framework to evaluate and develop your own capabilities."

PHILIP MORGAN REES

Head of Wealth Management and Advice, Milford Asset Management

"In today's fast-paced AI-enhanced world, this easy-to-read book emphasises the importance of the advisor-client relationship. It demonstrates how we can build deeper trust and more rewarding relationships by embracing the tools in the Bionic Adviser. This book is a must-read for anyone seeking the best outcomes for their clients."

LINDA STURGESS

Master of Technological Futures

THE BIONIC ADVISOR

Andrew MacDonald, PhD

PRIVACY AND CONFIDENTIALITY DISCLAIMER

PROTECTING CLIENT TRUST AND CONFIDENTIALITY

Throughout this book, I share insights, case studies, and practical examples drawn from three decades of experience advising clients across global financial services, sovereign wealth funds, family offices, and professional services firms. These real-world examples form the foundation of the frameworks and methodologies presented.

CLIENT PRIVACY AND CONFIDENTIALITY

In keeping with the highest standards of professional confidentiality and client privacy, I have deliberately chosen not to use actual client names, company names, or identifying details in any case studies or examples. All client references have been anonymised, with specific details modified or generalised to protect individual and institutional privacy while preserving the strategic and practical value of the lessons learned. The cases presented are composites drawn from multiple engagements, with identifying characteristics altered to ensure complete confidentiality. Where geographical or industry context is relevant to the strategic insight, I have retained this information only when it does not compromise client anonymity.

PROFESSIONAL STANDARDS

This approach reflects the foundational principle that trust, the central theme of this book, must be earned and maintained through unwavering commitment to confidentiality. The frameworks, methodologies, and insights shared here are no less valuable for being presented without attribution; indeed, they demonstrate that the principles of Bionic Advisory excellence transcend any single client or engagement.

ACKNOWLEDGMENT OF SOURCES

While I cannot name specific clients, I remain deeply grateful to the executives, boards, and advisory teams who have partnered with me in developing and refining these approaches. Their willingness to embrace transformation and their commitment to building trust-based, AI-augmented advisory capabilities have made this work possible. The insights in this book belong to the collective wisdom of the global advisory community, presented here to advance the practice of trusted advisory services in the age of artificial intelligence.

ISBN 978-1-7643342-0-4

Written by: Andrew MacDonald, PhD
Book design by: Bradley Graham

bionicadvisor.ai

For the clients who push me to
continually create and innovate,

the friends who encourage
me along the way,

and above all my family,
whose belief, love and support
make everything possible.

CONTENTS

FOREWORD

It begins quietly.

A sovereign fund executive in the Middle East confides that she no longer asks her senior advisors for investment outlooks. She can generate fifty scenarios herself using AI. A family office director in London admits he trusts his algorithm more than his private banker. A global CEO tells me he values his advisor's judgement, but only if it is backed by data, he can interrogate himself.

These aren't isolated moments. They are signals. Signals that the old foundations of advisory (information advantage, expertise held close, reputation built on exclusivity) are collapsing in real time.

And yet, in that collapse lies an unprecedented opportunity.

Because what clients are truly searching for is not more

information. They are drowning in that. What they seek is someone **who can help them see clearly, decide confidently, and act with courage in a world of accelerating complexity.** They want an advisor who can stand at the intersection of empathy and machine intelligence, and who can weave the two together in a way that multiplies trust.

That is the promise of this book.

THE READER'S CHALLENGE

If you are reading these pages, you are likely an advisor, consultant, or executive already under pressure. You know your clients have more tools than ever. You know they are questioning fees, loyalty, and even the necessity of having an advisor. You sense that trust is harder to earn and easier to lose.

You also know (if you are honest) that AI is no longer something you can delegate to the tech team or the "innovation lab." It is here, in your conversations, shaping your credibility. It is in the hands of your clients, reshaping their expectations.

The challenge is not whether AI will transform advisory. It already has. The challenge is whether you will adapt, whether you will become **bionic**.

WHY THIS BOOK MATTERS NOW

Advisory and professional services are standing at the most consequential crossroads in their history.

On one path are those who cling to the traditional model: protecting information, repeating legacy processes, reassuring clients with old credentials. That path leads to irrelevance.

On the other path are those who reimagine themselves as **Bionic Advisors:** professionals who leverage AI to deliver faster insights, deeper foresight, and more personalised engagement than either could achieve alone. This path leads not only to survival but to a new era of growth, influence, and trust at scale.

This book is your guide to the second path.

It will show you how to:

- Recognise and overcome the **collapse of traditional advantages**.
- Master the **Bionic Trust Equation**, the framework that adapts the timeless principles of credibility, reliability, intimacy, and orientation for the AI age.
- Apply the Trust Multipliers (problem finding, mindset mastery, authentic connection) that transform every client interaction.
- Use the **30-Day Bionic Assessment** to lay the foundations for your own transition.
- Prepare to transform your practice into a **bionic enterprise** capable of orchestrating trust and intelligence across teams, clients, and ecosystems.

WHAT YOU CAN EXPECT

This is not an academic treatise. It is a practitioner's guide, forged in real engagements with wealth managers, consultants, sovereign funds, and executives across Asia, the Middle East, Europe, and the Americas. You will find case studies, tools, and stories. You will also find provocations.

Some of what you read here may unsettle you. That is intentional. The advisors who will thrive in the years ahead are not those who double down on comfort zones. They are those who are willing to experiment, to fail, to reimagine themselves, and to lead their clients through uncertainty with confidence.

A PERSONAL NOTE

For more than three decades, I have worked alongside advisors, consultants, and executives navigating change. I have seen how fragile trust can be, and how powerful it becomes when multiplied. I have also seen how quickly clients recognise authenticity, empathy, and courage when they encounter them.

Technology will never replace those human qualities. But those human qualities, without the amplification of technology, will no longer be enough.

The advisors who win the future are those who understand that **AI does not diminish humanity. It demands a deeper humanity**.

YOUR JOURNEY BEGINS

So, as you turn the page, ask yourself:

- Am I prepared to let go of the old sources of advantage that no longer serve me?
- Am I ready to embrace new ways of building trust, ways that combine empathy, foresight, and machine intelligence?
- Am I willing to become more than an expert, more than a consultant, more than a professional? Am I willing to become **bionic**?

This book will not just show you how. It will challenge you to step into that identity. Because in the end, when every client has access to infinite intelligence, only those who can multiply trust will truly matter. The future will not belong to the traditional advisor, nor to the machine.

The future belongs to the Bionic Advisor.

INTRODUCTION

Your AI Advantage Starts Now.

By the end of this book, you will have completed a comprehensive readiness assessment to become a Bionic Advisor. You will be capable of multiplying trust, scaling impact, and creating competitive advantages through AI amplification. This comprehensive readiness assessment reveals current capabilities across three specific Trust Multiplier areas and identifies exactly where advisors stand relative to both traditional approaches and fully automated advisory solutions. Through systematic 30-day evaluation, the process creates a personalised transformation roadmap whilst identifying highest-impact client relationship opportunities.

In late 2024, I was facilitating an executive education workshop in London for members of a Middle Eastern royal family when the conversation turned to a familiar topic. We were discussing alternative investment strategies during lunch when one of the participants, a senior family office director, joined the conversation. Andrew," he said, "my nephew just used AI to analyse our entire portfolio in minutes and identified opportunities we've been overlooking for years. I'm starting to wonder, what exactly are we paying our advisors for?

The conversation that ensued lasted for nearly an hour. Here were some of the world's most sophisticated investors, served by some of the world's leading wealth management firms, suddenly questioning the fundamental value proposition that had defined their relationships for decades.

That moment crystallised what I've witnessed over the past 18 months: the most fundamental disruption to hit professional services since the internet transformed how we access and share information. This isn't about technology adoption or process improvement. This is about the complete redefinition of what it means to create and capture value as a trusted advisor in an age where artificial intelligence can process more information, identify more patterns, and generate more insights than any advisor ever could.

WHAT YOU'LL DISCOVER THROUGH THIS ASSESSMENT

This book will guide you through a comprehensive evaluation that reveals three critical readiness areas through assessment of the Trust Multiplier Framework.

Trust Multiplier #1: Problem Finder, Not Problem Solver

Trust Multiplier #2: Client Mindset Master

Trust Multiplier #3: Authentic Connector Who Builds Trust

These three capabilities, explored in detail in Chapter 2, form the foundation of your competitive advantage as a Bionic Advisor.

THE PROFESSIONAL SERVICES RECKONING

The data tells a story that can no longer be ignored. Boston Consulting Group's latest research reveals that AI remains a top priority for business leaders worldwide in 2025, with a strong focus on generating tangible results. [1] Yet their studies also show that 74% of companies struggle to achieve and scale value from AI adoption, [2] creating a massive opportunity for advisors who can bridge this implementation gap.

Across every industry that I have consulted to (banking, management consulting, legal services, engineering, government and beyond) the same pattern emerges. Traditional competitive advantages are not just eroding; they've become obsolete. The information asymmetry that once justified premium fees has vanished. The analysis that once took weeks now happens in hours. The insights that once required decades of experience are being generated by algorithms that never sleep, never forget, and continuously learn from millions of data points.

Yet here's what the "AI will replace everything" narrative misses: the most successful advisory professionals aren't being replaced by artificial intelligence. They're being amplified by it. They've discovered how to multiply their most sought-after capabilities (judgement, empathy, creativity, and relationship-building) through AI enhancement rather than being rendered obsolete by AI competition.

THE EMERGENCE OF THE BIONIC ADVISOR

Through my work with advisory professionals across professional and financial services, I've identified a new category of advisors who are not just surviving but thriving in the AI era. I call them Bionic Advisors (professionals who have mastered the art of amplifying their own judgement with intelligence rather than competing against it).

These advisors have cracked the code on what I call the Trust Multiplier Framework: three fundamental capabilities that distinguish Bionic Advisors from both traditional practitioners and pure AI systems. They've learned to multiply trust rather than simply build it, creating competitive advantages that neither advisor expertise alone nor AI alone could achieve.

WHAT IS A BIONIC ADVISOR?

The term "Bionic Advisor" may evoke images of science fiction (half human, half machine, operating with superhuman capabilities). Perhaps even Jaime Sommers or Steve Austin. But it represents a new archetype of trusted professional, one who blends deep professional insight with powerful machine intelligence to deliver better, faster, and more personalised advice than was ever possible before.

This isn't about replacing the advisor with algorithms. It's about transforming the very nature of advice itself. A Bionic Advisor integrates the irreplaceable qualities of their experience with the precision, scale, and foresight offered by artificial intelligence, data analytics, and automation. In doing so, they become more trusted, not less.

In our work across wealth management, consulting, legal services, and government advisory, we have witnessed a powerful pattern emerge. Advisors who lean into this fusion of human and machine, of art and science, outperform their peers. They engage deeper with clients. They convert uncertainty into opportunity. They deliver clarity in complexity. And most importantly, they earn trust in ways that legacy models of advice can no longer replicate.

So let me define it clearly: A Bionic Advisor is a professional who consciously integrates judgement, empathy, creativity and expertise with AI-driven insights to enhance trust, scale impact, and elevate the quality of advice.

They are human-in-the-loop by design, not by default. They choose where to automate, where to augment, and where to deeply humanise. They don't chase the latest technology for its own sake. They use it intentionally, creating experiences and designing systems that enhance their judgement, not obscure it.

THE PHILOSOPHY BEHIND BIONIC ADVISORY

This is not just a technical evolution. It's a philosophical one. Traditional advisors are trained to problem-solve and provide answers. Bionic Advisors are trained to craft better questions, to iterate potential solutions, to frame better decisions, and to co-create value with clients who themselves are more informed, more empowered, and often more sceptical than ever before.

Importantly, a Bionic Advisor isn't just someone who uses a CRM with some AI features or reads a dashboard of predictive insights. Tools are meaningless without intent. What defines a Bionic Advisor is mindset, not just technology.

BIONIC ADVISORS IN PRACTICE

We have seen Bionic Advisors:

- Deploy machine learning algorithms to analyse portfolio

risk across multiple asset classes, enabling wealth managers to move from quarterly to more frequent rebalancing recommendations based on real-time market conditions
- Automate due diligence processes for private equity deals by combining AI document analysis with human judgement, reducing initial screening time from weeks to days whilst maintaining investment committee standards
- Apply natural language processing to review regulatory compliance across client communications, allowing compliance officers to identify potential issues within hours rather than months during regulatory audits
- Implement predictive analytics to identify clients at risk of moving their assets, enabling relationship managers to proactively address concerns and improve retention rates
- Deploy robo-advisory platforms enhanced with human oversight for mass affluent clients, expanding service provision to previously underserved market segments whilst maintaining personalised advisory standards

In each case, the advisor's expertise is enhanced, not replaced. Technology handles data processing and pattern recognition, whilst advisors focus on relationship building, strategic thinking, and complex decision-making.

The rise of the Bionic Advisor represents a fundamental shift in professional service delivery. Rather than competing with artificial intelligence, successful advisors are learning to orchestrate human-AI partnerships that deliver superior client outcomes. They become more valuable by becoming more collaborative, combining technological efficiency with advisor insight and trust.

—

THE TRUST MULTIPLIER FRAMEWORK: YOUR COMPETITIVE EDGE

Through my research across thousands of client engagements, I've identified that the advisors who will dominate the next decade have already begun developing three critical Trust Multiplier capabilities that distinguish Bionic Advisors from both traditional practitioners and pure AI systems.

These advisors have learned to multiply trust rather than simply build it, creating competitive advantages that neither advisor expertise alone nor AI alone could achieve. The complete Trust Multiplier Framework, including detailed assessment guidance and case studies, is covered comprehensively in Chapter 2.

THE TRANSFORMATION IMPERATIVE

The window for competitive advantage isn't just closing (it's slamming shut at unprecedented speed). The firms that move first aren't just gaining market share; they're establishing positions that will be impossible to challenge.

The transformation is happening across every sector. Where traditional research and development processes might take years and cost hundreds of millions, new AI-enhanced approaches are delivering results in months at a fraction of the cost. The firms that hesitate aren't just falling behind; they're watching newcomers leapfrog decades of accumulated advantage.

THE EVIDENCE FROM THE FIELD

My work with advisory professionals has revealed that the transformation from trusted advisor to Bionic Advisor follows predictable patterns. The most successful transitions happen when advisors understand that AI amplifies rather than replaces their knowledge, expertise, and capabilities.

In my research on client experience, I've found that the challenge isn't simply technological (it's deeply human). As I documented in my London Business School Review article, the fundamental issue facing financial institutions is that "banks are all similar. It comes down to the private banker, how he or she manages you, what insights they offer you and how genuine they are in wanting to have you as a client"[3]. The advisors who are winning aren't those with the most sophisticated AI tools, but those who use AI to become more genuinely helpful, more insightfully prepared, and more authentically connected to their clients' real needs.

YOUR READINESS ASSESSMENT AND DEVELOPMENT PATHWAY

This book provides a comprehensive framework for assessing your current capabilities and creating your transformation roadmap from traditional trusted advisor to Bionic Advisor through evaluation of the Trust Multiplier Framework.

Complete assessment tools and personalised evaluation frameworks are available at bionicadvisor.ai.

Chapter 1: Why AI Won't Replace You (But AI-Powered Advisors Will Replace You)

Understand the competitive crisis through real-world evidence and discover why Bionic Advisors win whilst traditional advisors lose.

Chapter 2: The Trust Multiplier Framework

Master the complete foundation for AI-era success. This chapter provides detailed guidance on developing each Trust Multiplier, complete with foundational insights, case studies, and your personal development roadmap.

Chapter 3:
Your 30-Day Bionic Readiness Assessment

Understand the systematic week-by-week evaluation framework that identifies Trust Multiplier strengths, capability gaps, and highest-impact development opportunities for becoming a Bionic Advisor.

Chapter 4:
Building Your High-Performance Bionic Practice

Scale your individual readiness insights to practice-level transformation planning through Trust Multiplier team assessment, systematic capability development frameworks, and competitive positioning strategies.

Chapter 5:
Leading Your Bionic Team

Build and lead high-performance teams that amplify Trust Multiplier capabilities across your organisation, with proven frameworks for coaching, culture development, and change management.

Chapter 6:
The Future of Bionic Advisory

Prepare for enterprise-level transformation with strategic guidance on ROI measurement, regulatory compliance, and sustainable competitive advantage through Trust Multiplier mastery.

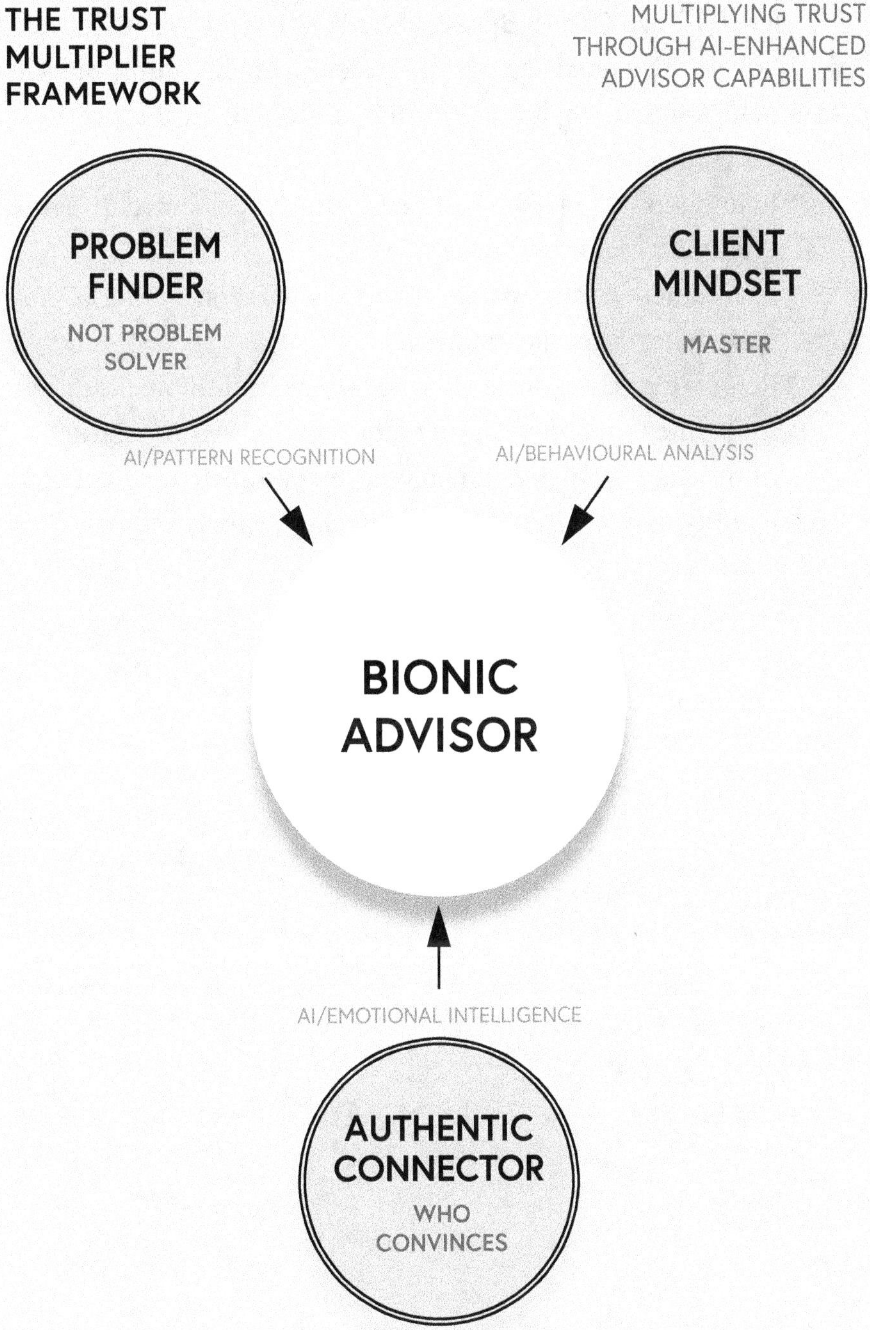
THE TRUST
MULTIPLIER
FRAMEWORK
MULTIPLYING TRUST
THROUGH AI-ENHANCED
ADVISOR CAPABILITIES
PROBLEM
FINDER
NOT PROBLEM
SOLVER
CLIENT
MINDSET
MASTER
AI/PATTERN RECOGNITION
AI/BEHAVIOURAL ANALYSIS
BIONIC
ADVISOR
AI/EMOTIONAL INTELLIGENCE
AUTHENTIC
CONNECTOR
WHO
CONVINCES

HOW TO USE THIS BOOK FOR MAXIMUM IMPACT

This book is designed as both strategic guide and practical assessment manual. Each chapter builds directly on the previous one and includes:

- Foundational insights to evaluate your current Trust Multiplier readiness
- Assessment frameworks with evaluation criteria for systematic capability analysis
- Real-world case studies from successful Bionic Advisor assessment and development journeys across industries
- Immediate evaluation steps you can complete now to begin identifying your competitive advantage opportunities

THE MOMENT OF TRUTH

The advisors who will dominate the landscape of 2030 are making their foundational decisions now. Those who delay will be studying these winners as case studies in business school disruption classes. The future belongs to the Bionic Advisor (those who understand that artificial intelligence becomes a competitive advantage only when it amplifies advisor judgement, never when it replaces it).

The same principle applies to all advisory professionals. As I've observed in my banking research, financial institutions "must evolve from pitching products and solutions to providing unique client experiences". [3] The question is not whether AI will transform advisory relationships, but whether you will lead or follow that transformation.

Your clients are ready. The technology is available. Your competitors are moving.

The only question is: will you act before it's too late?

Let's begin your transformation.

For readers seeking advanced implementation tools, personalised assessments, and community support, comprehensive resources are available at bionicadvisor.ai

CHAPTER 1

Why AI Won't Replace You (But AI-Powered Advisors Will Replace You)

The Moment Everything Changed

The laptop screen flickered to life with the quiet confidence of someone about to shatter everything I thought I knew about the future of advisory services. We were at a financial services conference in London in late 2024, during a panel on "AI in Professional Advisory Services." The morning session had just concluded when one of my clients, a senior partner at a multinational engineering advisory firm, approached my table during the networking break.

"Andrew," she said, opening her laptop, "you need to see what just happened to our profession."

What appeared on screen was a comprehensive financial analysis that took my breath away: a detailed investment proposal for a complex international acquisition, complete with risk assessments, regulatory compliance reviews across multiple jurisdictions, tax optimisation strategies, and post-acquisition integration planning. The level of detail was extraordinary: sophisticated financial modelling, comprehensive due diligence summaries, and strategic recommendations that accounted for market volatility, regulatory changes, and post-acquisition synergies.

I found myself studying the analysis with the mixture of admiration and professional concern that only comes from recognising work that matches anything in the best advisory firms' portfolios. The financial modelling was sophisticated, the analysis comprehensive, the integration of multiple advisory disciplines masterful. This was the calibre of work that defines world-class advisory relationships.

"This is remarkable," I said, meaning every word. "How long did this take your team?"

Her expression shifted, and I recognised something I would soon understand completely: a combination of amazement and concern that comes from watching the foundational assumptions of your career dissolve in real time.

"That's exactly the problem, Andrew. Our advisory team didn't create this. Our new AI platform generated this complete proposal in less than three hours."

The silence that followed felt like standing at the edge of a professional cliff I hadn't known existed. Here was a professional who had built her reputation on advisory excellence, who had spent two decades mastering the complex interplay of financial analysis, strategic thinking, and client relationships that define modern advisory services. And she was watching an AI system accomplish in hours what had traditionally required multidisciplinary teams working for weeks.

But what she said next changed everything: 'The real question isn't whether AI will replace our engineers. It's whether we, as advisors, can evolve fast enough to stay relevant when our clients realise what's possible without our involvement'."

That conversation wasn't an isolated incident. It was a symptom of a transformation that's already reshaping the advisory landscape at unprecedented speed. While most advisors are still debating whether AI will affect their industry, the revolution has already begun.

THE COLLAPSE OF TRADITIONAL ADVANTAGES

The speed and depth of change in the advisory landscape has created a moment when traditional advantages become liabilities overnight. The firms that built their reputations on information asymmetry, exclusive access, and advisor-only expertise are discovering that these advantages are not just disappearing – they have already vanished.

For decades, advisory firms commanded premium fees through privileged access to information. Investment banks had market intelligence unavailable elsewhere. Consulting firms possessed proprietary benchmarking data. Wealth managers offered exclusive research and early investment access.

AI has shattered these information monopolies completely. Financial data can now be processed by AI systems in real-time. Industry insights are being replicated by machine learning algorithms that analyse millions of data points simultaneously. Investment opportunities are being democratised through AI platforms that identify prospects across global markets.

The transformation is happening faster than most industry leaders anticipated. According to McKinsey's latest State of AI report, 78% of respondents say their organisations use AI in at least one business function, up from 55% a year earlier. [1] This represents a dramatic acceleration, with generative AI leading the charge. Research from Wharton's AI program shows that weekly usage of generative AI has nearly doubled from 37% in 2023 to 72% in 2024.[2]

Traditional advisory processes that once demonstrated thoroughness now signal inefficiency. The three-week analysis cycle that showed diligence in 2020 suggests incompetence in 2025. Clients working with AI-augmented competitors receive comprehensive analysis in days, not weeks.

The investment in AI infrastructure continues to accelerate, with enterprises increasingly recognising that AI adoption is no longer optional but essential for competitive survival. This massive shift in resource allocation is accelerating the development of AI capabilities that will continue to reshape client expectations.

THE COST OF PARALYSIS

Across the advisory landscape, executives find themselves overwhelmed by the pace of change. They recognise the potential of AI but struggle with implementation strategies. They understand the competitive threat but lack frameworks for response.

This paralysis is costly. Research indicates that more than 80 percent of AI projects fail, with implementation challenges rather than technological limitations serving as the primary barrier to successful deployment and scaling.[3] The firms succeeding aren't choosing between human expertise and artificial intelligence, they're creating competitive advantages through strategic integration of both capabilities.

The transformation isn't coming – it's already here. But many advisors are falling behind in implementation. The challenge is no longer simply understanding AI's capabilities; it's developing the agility and mindset to adapt before the market moves on without you.

THE UNPRECEDENTED OPPORTUNITY

The conversation raging in advisory firms today fundamentally misunderstands the future. Partners argue about whether to embrace AI or resist it. Teams divide into camps: those who see AI as a threat to human expertise and those who view it as an inevitable replacement for human judgment.

They're fighting the wrong war. The future doesn't belong to AI or advisors; it belongs to the Bionic Advisors who multiply trust through advisor-AI partnerships.

As industry leaders consistently obscrvc: ‘AI is not going to replace humans, but humans with AI are going to replace humans without AI."[4]

This convergence of thinking from leaders across industries signals a fundamental shift towards human-AI collaboration as the dominant paradigm for workplace evolution. The firms winning in this new landscape have discovered something remarkable: AI doesn't diminish the human elements of advisory relationships – it amplifies them.

Through my work with wealth management clients, we're transforming client advisory and portfolio management processes without replacing human expertise. We've helped deploy AI systems that handle data analysis, risk assessment, and preliminary portfolio analysis whilst empowering human advisors to focus on relationship building and complex decision-making. The result demonstrates what industry leaders advocate: technology that amplifies human capability rather than replacing it. Advisors who collaborate with AI can deliver unprecedented value:

Faster insights: Real-time data analysis combined with advisor interpretation provides clients with immediate, contextualised intelligence instead of waiting weeks for traditional research cycles.

Predictive foresight: AI pattern recognition across vast datasets, validated by advisor knowledge, identifies emerging opportunities and risks before they become obvious to the market.

Mass-personalisation at scale: Behavioural analytics combined with advisor empathy enables hyper-personalisation for multiple clients simultaneously, breaking the traditional trade-off between breadth and depth of service.

Deeper trust through empathy plus data: AI-driven analysis reduces cognitive bias whilst transparent decision-making processes build confidence, allowing advisors to focus on the human elements that create lasting client relationships.

Early movers are already capturing market share by implementing these capabilities systematically rather than experimenting with isolated AI tools.

STANDING ON THE SHOULDERS OF GIANTS

Before we dive into this transformation, we need to acknowledge the foundation we're building upon. An entire generation of consultants, financial advisors, and professional service providers have been guided by David Maister's groundbreaking work "The Trusted Advisor."[5] His Trust Equation became the gold standard for understanding how advisory relationships create and maintain trust:

Trust = (Credibility + Reliability + Intimacy) ÷ Self-Orientation

Maister's insights remain profoundly relevant. Trust is still the foundation of every advisory relationship. Clients still seek advisors who combine deep knowledge with genuine empathy for their outcomes. Sustainable advisory practices still require systematic approaches to earning and maintaining client trust.

But when "The Trusted Advisor" was published in 2000, the advisory world operated under fundamentally different constraints. Information was scarce and expensive to obtain. Client analysis required weeks of research by large teams. Market insights came from professional networks and institutional relationships built over decades.

Maister's trust equation was perfectly calibrated for that environment. But AI has fundamentally altered every component of his framework, and we need to evolve our approach accordingly.

WHEN TRUST MEETS TECHNOLOGY

Consider how AI has transformed each element of Maister's trust equation:

Credibility can no longer rely solely on advisor expertise when AI systems process decades of market data in seconds, identify patterns across global datasets simultaneously, and generate predictive insights with unprecedented accuracy.

Reliability once meant delivering consistent outcomes within reasonable time constraints. But AI systems offer 24/7 availability, instant response times, and analysis that never fluctuates based on mood, fatigue, or cognitive bias.

Intimacy traditionally forced a cruel trade-off between

personalisation and scale. You could serve many clients adequately or few clients exceptionally, but not both. AI analytics now enable hyper-personalisation at scale through behavioural pattern recognition, predictive modelling, and real-time customisation.

Self-Orientation becomes more complex when recommendations emerge from AI rather than direct advisor judgment. Whilst AI can eliminate many forms of bias, it raises new questions about transparency, explainability, and accountability in advisory relationships.

THE BIONIC TRUST EQUATION

$$\text{Trust multiplier} = \frac{\text{Enchanced credibility} + \text{AI Fluency} + \text{Scaled intimacy}}{\text{Amplified self orientation}}$$

ENCHANCED CREDIBILITY

AI powered analysis + advisor expertise

AI FLUENCY

Seamless integration of AI insights

SCALED INTIMACY

Hyper personalised at scale

AMPLIFIED SELF-ORIENTATION

AI systems can amply self-orientation

The Bionic Advisor model doesn't discard Maister's framework – it evolves it for an AI-enhanced world. Every principle that made the original Trust Equation powerful remains essential, but each component must be reimagined to harness AI capabilities whilst preserving the advisor capabilities clients value most.

This framework reveals how each element of advisory trust evolves rather than disappears in the AI era. Enhanced Credibility moves beyond traditional expertise demonstrations to AI-augmented analytical capabilities that provide clients with deeper insights and superior outcomes. The shift recognises that information democratisation has moved competitive advantage from exclusive access to superior analysis and contextualisation. AI Fluency represents the transparent and effective use of artificial intelligence to enhance client value, ensuring that technology serves client outcomes rather than advisor convenience. Scaled Intimacy combines AI's analytical capabilities with human empathy to deliver personalised understanding that transcends traditional limitations of time and resource constraints. However, the most critical evolution lies in recognising how Amplified Self-Orientation can undermine everything else. In the AI era, self-serving behaviours become magnified through black box algorithms and opaque processes, making transparency about AI usage and genuine commitment to client success more essential than ever.

THE 30-DAY ASSESSMENT WINDOW

The competitive landscape is shifting faster than most advisors realise. Early adopters are establishing market positions that will be increasingly difficult to challenge, whilst traditional firms lose ground daily. Based on analysis of successful Bionic Advisor development, advisors have a critical window, approximately 30 days, to complete their readiness assessment and create their transformation roadmap before competitors establish unassailable advantages.

This development process starts with systematic capability assessment and strategic planning, not waiting for institutional change or market clarity. It begins with evaluating current AI readiness and identifying specific opportunities to enhance client value within your current role.

THE CHOICE THAT DEFINES EVERYTHING

The evidence is overwhelming: AI won't replace human advisors, but AI-powered advisors will replace traditional advisors who fail to adapt. The transformation is happening now, not in some distant future.

The partner's insight proves prophetic: "The real question isn't whether AI can replace what we do. It's whether we, as advisors, can evolve fast enough to stay relevant when our clients realise what's possible without our direct involvement."

Clients have already experienced what's possible. They're choosing AI-augmented advisors over traditional expertise at accelerating rates. The question isn't whether this transformation will happen, it's whether you'll lead or follow it.

In the next 30 days, you'll either begin building the bionic capabilities that multiply your value to clients, or you'll watch competitors make your traditional expertise irrelevant. There is no middle ground. There is no "wait and see." There is only the decision to evolve or become irrelevant.

Your clients aren't waiting for you to figure this out. They're already experiencing what AI-augmented advisory relationships can deliver. Every day you delay is another day your competitors establish unassailable advantages in the minds of the clients you

THE ADVISORY COMPETITION LANDSCAPE

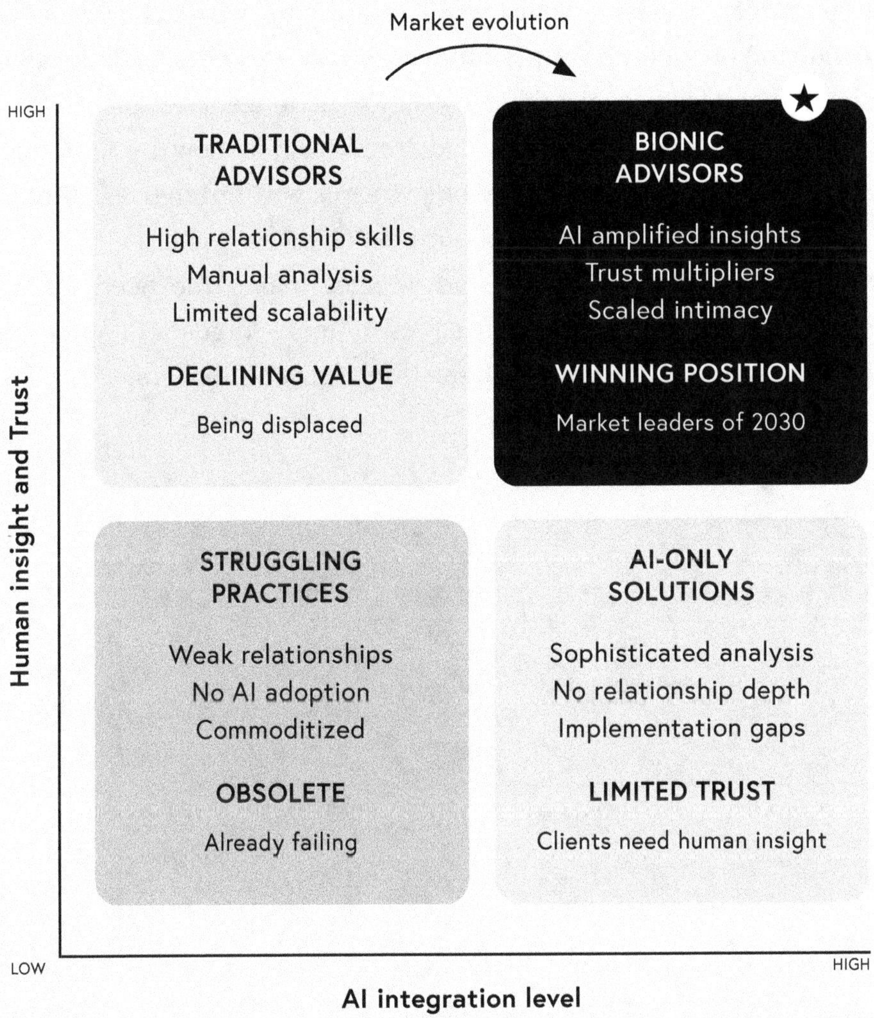

The Bionic Advisor combines the best of human insights and AI capabilities

thought were loyal.

The transformation from trusted advisor to Bionic Advisor isn't just about survival, it's about seizing the greatest competitive opportunity in advisory history. The advisors who act now will define the next decade of their industry. The ones who hesitate will spend that decade explaining why they're no longer relevant.

To seize this opportunity, advisors need a new system for multiplying trust. That framework is explained through the three Trust Multipliers, the subject of our next chapter

The erosion of traditional advantages makes the need for a structured system to build trust even more urgent. Chapter 2 introduces that system through the three Trust Multipliers.

CHAPTER 2

Mastering the Three Trust Multipliers That Make AI Work for You

The Question That Changes Everything.

Harald Meier, Managing Director of a management consulting firm headquartered in Zurich, had just delivered his most successful quarter in the competitive management consulting market. Every metric including client retention rates, project completion timelines, and realisation rates, reflected exactly what industry research predicted: meaningful productivity gains and superior client outcomes when AI augments consulting capabilities.

But the question his Managing Partner posed that morning revealed a deeper challenge: "Harald, your results are impressive, but we need to discuss something beyond the numbers. We have over 200 consultants across Europe. If we scale your approach beyond Switzerland, are we simply improving efficiency, or are we fundamentally changing how clients experience and trust us?"

This moment reveals the critical gap between AI implementation and transformation. Individual AI adoption proves technology can enhance consulting capabilities. But scaling that success requires understanding something far more profound: how artificial intelligence multiplies trust, rather than merely improving productivity.

THE EXECUTIVE PARALYSIS PROBLEM

The answer emerged from a troubling pattern observed across professional services. Despite having access to more sophisticated analysis than ever before, C-suite executives were increasingly paralysed by choice and overwhelmed by information complexity.

"We have more data at our fingertips than ever before. But it can be overwhelming. Executives can end up wallowing in it, "saying, 'Why don't we do a little more analysis?' or 'Can't we look at this a different way?' ... Analysis paralysis" is a big driver of indecision," explains Michael A. Roberto, Trustee Professor of Management at Bryant University, describing the decision-making fatigue plaguing today's C-Suite. [1]

Research by Professor Sheena Iyengar at Columbia Business School demonstrates that excessive choice creates decision paralysis. In her landmark study, she found that when faced with too many options, people often choose nothing at all. As Iyengar explains, "The more choices you give people, the more likely you are to either confuse them, or to freeze them. And the more they freeze, the more likely they are to walk away."[2]

This wasn't occurring because clients lacked trusted advisors.

They were experiencing what cognitive scientists identify as information overload, a state where sophisticated analysis exceeded their capacity to process and act upon it. Nobel Prize winner Herbert Simon captured this perfectly: "A wealth of information creates a poverty of attention."[3]

The consulting industry had inadvertently created this problem. Advisors were analytically brilliant, relationship-focused, and deeply committed to client success. But they operated in an environment where traditional consulting delivery was drowning clients in data complexity.

This revelation forced a fundamental question: In an age of artificial intelligence, why should any C-suite executive trust your advice?

THE COMPLETE TRUST MULTIPLIER FRAMEWORK

The solution emerged from studying what already worked: analysing behavioural patterns of top-performing management consultants across professional services. My research conducted with advisory professionals since 2008 reveals that the highest-performing consultants consistently exhibit three capabilities that become exponentially more powerful when enhanced by AI, creating multiplicative rather than additive value.

Trust Multiplier #1: Problem Finders, Not Problem Solvers

The highest-performing consultants don't wait for clients to identify strategic challenges; they anticipate disruptions before clients recognise them. Traditional consultants gather information about known problems. Exceptional consultants help executives discover strategic blind spots they didn't know existed.

In a recent consulting engagement with a Middle Eastern sovereign fund, the executive team had engaged me to create a new client and account management framework. While most consultants would have delivered exactly that, I instead surfaced a hidden vulnerability: the fund's exposure to clients who did not align with their stated ESG objectives, something not on the Board's radar. By conducting full analysis of their major client accounts, we reframed the challenge from account management to long-term competitive positioning.

This wasn't reactive consulting; it was finding problems that reveal strategic blind spots clients don't yet see but can't afford to ignore.

As Clayton Christensen observed in 'The Innovator's Dilemma', "The reason why it is so difficult for existing firms to capitalise on disruptive innovations is that their processes and their business model that make them good at the existing business make them bad at competing for the disruption." [4]

AI AMPLIFICATION: PATTERN RECOGNITION ACROSS EXPONENTIAL DATA

Consider Harald's insights during his readiness assessment. His highest-value client, an insurance company, was unknowingly exposed to significant competitive disruption from an emerging market player. Traditional analysis would have required months of market research across multiple regions.

AI analysis identified the threat in days, processing real-time patent filings, funding announcements, talent acquisition patterns, and regulatory changes across 15 countries simultaneously. The system revealed that five seemingly unrelated startups were part of a coordinated insure-tech ecosystem attacking the client's core market position.

But AI didn't replace Harald's strategic thinking; it amplified it. The technology processed exponentially more data and identified subtle patterns, but Harald provided the strategic interpretation that transformed raw analysis into actionable competitive intelligence.

FROM HUMAN-IN-THE-LOOP TO ADVISOR-IN-THE-LOOP

The concept of "advisor-in-the-loop" builds directly on the established AI principle of "human-in-the-loop" (HITL) but adapts it specifically for professional advisory relationships. Human-in-the-loop is an iterative feedback process whereby a human (or team) interacts with an algorithmically generated system, involving human involvement in machine learning workflows to reduce errors and improve model performance. [5]

The human-in-the-loop approach reframes an automation problem as a Human-Computer Interaction (HCI) design problem, broadening the question from "how do we build a smarter system?" to "how do we incorporate useful, meaningful human interaction into the system?"

In the consulting context, this becomes "advisor-in-the-loop", where experienced consultants remain central to the AI-enhanced advisory process, providing strategic interpretation, client relationship management, and contextual judgment that transforms raw AI analysis into implementable client insights.

ADVISOR-IN-THE-LOOP: HUMAN-AI COLLABORATION MODEL

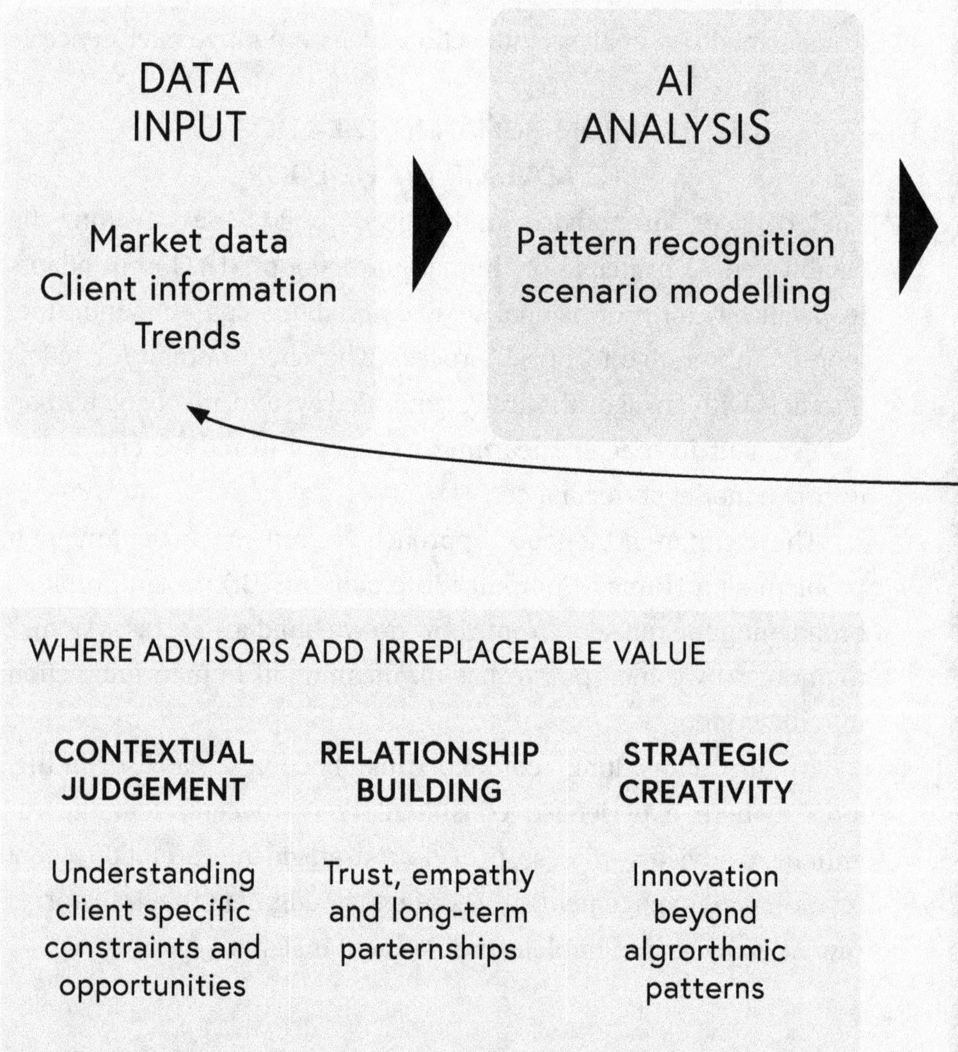

ADVISOR INTERPRETATION

Context
Judgement

CLIENT ENGAGEMENT

Strategic dialogue

Continuous Learning and Refinement

KEY INSIGHT:
AI Amplifies, Advisors Orchestrate

Artifical intelligence processes data and identifies patterns

Human advisors provide context, build trust and guide strategic decisions

Together, they multiply client value beyond what either could achieve alone

Case Study: Harald Meier's Strategic Transformation

Harald Meier assessed his readiness for transforming his consulting firm by combining AI-enabled strategic analysis with enhanced advisory skills. Instead of waiting for clients to ask, he pioneered quarterly "Strategic Horizon Conversations," leveraging AI to surface early competitive shifts, regulatory changes, and emerging market dynamics.

Before AI enhancement, Harald's relationships were transactional. Clients would engage his firm for specific projects and select winning proposals based primarily on price, viewing all firms as essentially the same.

After implementing Trust Multiplier #1, he guided clients through 360° strategic check-ins, uncovering blind spots like emerging supply chain disruptions or new Insurtech threats well before they became urgent. The shift moved their focus from immediate operational concerns to forward-looking strategic horizons, a transformation that took less than 18 months.

Trust Multiplier #2:
Client Mindset Masters

Exceptional consultants understand that executive decision-making operates at the intersection of rational analysis and intense personal pressure. They recognise that C-suite leaders navigate competing stakeholder demands whilst managing their own career risks, making every strategic recommendation a deeply personal calculation for the executive involved.

This capability represents the marriage of psychological insight and business acumen that separates transformational advisors from mere problem-solvers.

THE CONSULTING INSIGHT: EXECUTIVE DECISION-MAKING IS BOTH RATIONAL AND EMOTIONAL

Research reveals the psychological reality behind boardroom decisions. Executives consistently balance analytical frameworks with emotional considerations, particularly when facing uncertainty. This dual-processing approach becomes more pronounced under pressure, with 67% of C-suite executives reporting higher stress levels entering 2025 compared to the previous year. [6]

Consider how this works in practice. A CFO evaluating a digital transformation proposal isn't merely assessing ROI projections. She's calculating career risk if the initiative fails, board reaction if costs overrun, and team morale if redundancies follow. A CEO considering market expansion weighs not just competitive advantage, but shareholder patience, media scrutiny, and personal legacy. Top consultants recognise these unspoken calculations and address them directly.

AI transforms this capability by analysing communication patterns, meeting dynamics, and decision histories to predict individual executive responses. Advanced systems can identify stress indicators in voice patterns, engagement metrics in presentations, and even preferred cognitive processing styles through interaction data. This enables consultants to tailor their approach to each executive's psychological profile and current state.

Case Study: Strategic Transformation at Singapore Tech Giant

Through my work with Harald, we discovered that his insurance client's digital transformation was stalled not by technical challenges but by the CFO's concerns about implementation costs disrupting quarterly earnings targets.

AI analysis revealed that the CFO consistently responded positively to phased implementation plans but showed resistance to comprehensive transformation proposals. The system identified that the CFO's communication patterns suggested anxiety about explaining large capital expenditures to the board.

Harald redesigned his recommendations, using AI to model how phased implementation would protect quarterly performance while achieving transformation objectives. The CFO's engagement increased dramatically, and the client approved the digital transformation in weeks rather than months.

The Result: What had been an eight-month stalled engagement became a multi-million dollar expanded relationship through understanding and addressing the CFO's specific concerns and communication preferences.

Trust Multiplier #3: Authentic Connectors Who Convince

Top-performing consultants connect strategic insights to executive action through compelling visualisation and storytelling. They are skilled communicators who use case studies, scenarios, and strategic narratives to convince C-suite executives about complex strategic recommendations.

This capability becomes crucial in the AI era because executives process visual information significantly faster than text-based analysis. As John Medina notes in "Brain Rules," "Vision trumps all other senses... We learn and remember best through pictures, not through written or spoken words alone."[7]

Research by Stanford's Graduate School of Business shows that executives who can visualise strategic outcomes are 65% more likely to commit to implementation. [8] The most persuasive consultants understand that data alone rarely drives strategic action; executives need to feel confident about recommendations before they'll risk resources implementing them.

AI transforms strategic communication by creating dynamic, interactive models that help executives understand complex strategic scenarios. Instead of static presentations, AI generates real-time simulations showing how different strategic choices would perform under various market conditions.

Case Study: Regional Expansion Strategy Success

When I first met Harald, his consulting team delivered sound strategic advice, but the format hadn't changed in years. Deck after deck of bullet points, market matrices, and cost curves. It was technically rigorous but emotionally flat. The C-suite tuned in, nodded politely, and often... did nothing. We reimagined the entire experience.

Together, we introduced a more immersive and personalised way to guide strategic decisions. Instead of static PowerPoint presentations, Harald began using AI-generated Strategic Future Scenarios. Powered by tools like Power BI, Alteryx and Tableau for data integration and visualisation, and GPT-4 for narrative simulation, these sessions brought strategy to life.

Executives could see, in real time, how different expansion moves, entering an adjacent vertical or reshaping product lines, would impact their market share, margin trajectory, and organisational stress points. Harald didn't just present findings; he told the story behind each path.

Within 12 months, engagement with senior executives rose dramatically. Clients stayed in the room longer, asked deeper questions, and began requesting Harald's input earlier in their planning cycles.

But the real breakthrough came from client feedback. In post-engagement surveys, executives said they felt more confident in their strategic decisions, citing not just the data, but the clarity of the rationale, the contextual relevance, and the realism of the AI-generated scenarios.

The Trust Equation Evolution

David Maister's Trust Equation, Trust = (Credibility + Reliability + Intimacy) ÷ Self-Orientation, became the gold standard for understanding advisory relationships.[9]

The Trust Multiplier Framework builds on this foundation:

Trust Multiplier = (Enhanced Credibility + AI Fluency + Scaled Intimacy) ÷ Amplified Self-Orientation

Enhanced Credibility combines AI-powered strategic analysis with conventional consulting expertise. Consultants integrate AI-driven market intelligence, competitive analysis, and predictive modelling with their strategic experience and industry knowledge.

AI Fluency represents the consultant's ability to seamlessly integrate AI-driven insights into client interactions while maintaining focus on client success. As Satya Nadella, CEO of Microsoft, observes, "AI is not about replacing human capability; it's about amplifying human capability and human potential". [10]

Scaled Intimacy leverages AI to provide highly personalised recommendations that surpass what individual advisors could achieve alone. By analysing extensive client data, AI identifies organisational patterns, decision-making styles, and implementation preferences, enabling advisors to deliver deeply personalised advice.

The Trust Multiplier Framework doesn't simply make consultants more efficient; it fundamentally transforms their capacity to create strategic value while building sustainable competitive advantages.

YOUR STRATEGIC TRANSFORMATION ROADMAP

Understanding the Trust Multiplier Framework requires honest assessment of your current capabilities across all three pillars. This evaluation provides the foundation for developing your personal transformation strategy.

Problem Finding Assessment:

- Do you consistently identify strategic challenges before they become critical issues?
- How effectively do you use analytical tools to anticipate client needs?
- Can you translate pattern recognition into strategic conversations?

Client Mindset Mastery Assessment:

- How deeply do you understand your clients' complete decision-making ecosystem?
- Do you personalise strategic recommendations based on individual stakeholder preferences?
- Can you anticipate optimal timing and approach for strategic communications?

Authentic Connection Assessment:

- How effectively do you communicate complex strategic insights through compelling narratives?
- Do your recommendations resonate with each executive's specific strategic context?
- Can you create strategic scenarios that inspire confident executive action?

CHAPTER 2 SUMMARY: FROM FRAMEWORK TO IMPLEMENTATION

The Trust Multiplier Framework represents more than upgrading your tech stack, it's a fundamental reimagining of how advisor-client relationships create value in an AI-augmented world. Through the three pillars of Problem Finding, Client Mindset Mastery, and Authentic Connection, consultants transform from transactional providers into trust multipliers who co-create exponential client value.

The advisor-in-the-loop principle ensures that advisors remain central to this transformation. AI amplifies analytical capabilities, but advisors provide the client experience, relationship context, and market knowledge that turn data into implementable insights.

Your Next Steps:

- Identify your strongest Trust Multiplier capabilities and the development opportunities that will enhance your effectiveness
- Choose your strategic focus: Select the Trust Multiplier that will create the most immediate impact for your practice
- Prepare for assessment: Chapter 3 will provide your complete 30-day readiness evaluation framework

The Trust Multiplier Framework provides your foundation for AI-era consulting readiness assessment. Chapter 3 shows you exactly how to evaluate each multiplier through a systematic 30-day process that moves you from understanding concepts to identifying your capability gaps and creating your strategic development roadmap.

Your journey from trusted advisor to Bionic Advisor begins with this assessment framework and accelerates through the evaluation system you'll discover in Chapter 3.

CHAPTER 3

Your 30-Day Bionic Transformation

Understanding Your Current Position Before Moving Forward. Marcus Chen stood alone in his Singapore office late one evening, staring at the email that would force him to confront an uncomfortable truth. The client's message was direct: they were switching to a fintech provider whose AI platform could assess complex credit scenarios in hours, while he struggled to process a single loan application in a week.

"This can't be happening," he thought, looking out at the empty open office below. But it was happening, and Marcus was far from alone in facing this challenge.

The email had arrived that morning in early 2025, when

Marcus still believed that his banker's client relationships provided sufficient competitive protection. He had barely glanced at it during his morning client calls, dismissing it as another piece of industry disruption he could weather through superior service. Only now, fifteen hours later, did he understand its implications for his career and his team's future.

Twenty years of banking expertise. Client relationships built on trust, understanding, and personal service. All suddenly vulnerable to algorithms that processed information continuously, analysed patterns across vast datasets, and generated recommendations without fatigue or bias.

"You're not going to believe this transformation," Marcus would write to me two months later. "Eight weeks ago, my team was convinced that AI would commoditise relationship banking and potentially eliminate many advisory roles. Today, we're implementing a systematic approach across our entire Asia-Pacific operation. The clarity we gained about our actual capabilities versus our perceived limitations exceeded all expectations."

But Marcus's breakthrough hadn't emerged from superior technology or expensive external consulting. It had developed through the 30-Day Bionic Readiness Assessment, a systematic evaluation framework that enables financial professionals to understand their AI integration readiness whilst identifying specific opportunities to enhance client relationships. What made his story instructive wasn't the sophistication of his eventual AI implementation, but how a banker who had never considered himself technically inclined discovered his potential for leveraging artificial intelligence to strengthen customer relationships through careful assessment of his existing capabilities and systematic identification of enhancement opportunities.

THE 30-DAY BIONIC READINESS ASSESSMENT TIMELINE

1

WEEK 1

—

Current Capability Assessment

2

WEEK 2

—

Client Relationship Readiness

3

WEEK 3

—

Communication and Influence Assessment

4

WEEK 4

—

Integration and implementation

ASSESSMENT MAPS TO TRUST MULTIPLIER DEVELOPMENT

PROBLEM FINDER	**CLIENT MINDSET MASTER**	**AUTHENTIC CONNECTOR**
Week 1 and 4 focus	Week 2 and 4 focus	Week 3 and 4 focus
AI Pattern recognition	Behavioural analysis	Enhanced storytelling

THE ASSESSMENT IMPERATIVE

The competitive reality facing professional advisors has shifted fundamentally. Research conducted by Harvard Business School studying 758 consultants at Boston Consulting Group found that those using AI completed tasks 25% faster with 40% higher quality results. [1] However, the study also revealed something more significant: successful AI integration followed two distinctive patterns that required fundamentally different approaches to human-AI collaboration.

Some professionals acted as 'Centaurs', dividing their solution-creation activities between AI and themselves. Others functioned as 'Cyborgs', completely integrating their task flow with AI through continuous interaction with the technology. Both approaches succeeded, but they demanded different mindsets about collaborative intelligence and different assessments of individual readiness for human-AI partnership. [2]

Simultaneously, research published in Harvard Business Review indicated that AI would transform more than 40% of all work activity, with the largest impact expected in banking, insurance, and professional services sectors.[3] The transformation isn't approaching - it's already reshaping how professionals create value for clients.

But the competitive advantage wasn't flowing to firms with the most sophisticated technology. It was going to those that had systematically assessed their readiness and developed strategic approaches to integrating AI capabilities whilst preserving the human elements that create client trust.

This reality became evident when organisations that approached AI as technology deployment rather than capability assessment experienced client relationship deterioration despite technical sophistication. Research indicates that more than 80%

of AI projects fail, with implementation challenges rather than technological limitations serving as the primary barrier to successful deployment. [4]

THE TRUST ASSESSMENT THAT CHANGES EVERYTHING

The breakthrough insight emerged from studying what separated successful AI adoptions from expensive failures. Traditional technology implementations focused on capabilities: what systems could do, how they processed information, what insights they generated. But advisory relationships aren't built on capabilities alone - they're built on trust, which requires systematic assessment before enhancement.

The firms achieving measurable results had discovered a fundamental truth: AI implementation either strengthened client relationships or damaged them, with limited middle ground. The difference wasn't the technology itself but how professionals assessed their readiness to integrate it into client interactions whilst maintaining trust.

Consider what happened during my initial work with Harald Meier, Managing Director of a management consulting firm in Switzerland. When we began, Harald was experiencing what he called "analytical paralysis." Meeting after meeting filled with sophisticated analysis, market frameworks, and strategic recommendations. The content was technically rigorous, but clients often struggled to implement the insights effectively.

"It felt repetitive," Harald confided during our initial assessment session. "Clients would engage with my presentations professionally, then request follow-up meetings to clarify implementation approaches they should have been discussing during our strategy sessions. Something fundamental wasn't working in how we were connecting analysis to action."

Harald's assessment revealed a different path entirely. Instead of focusing on more sophisticated analysis, we evaluated how AI could enhance his ability to identify problems clients couldn't see independently, his understanding of how clients made strategic decisions, and his capability to connect insights to action through compelling narratives that drove implementation.

The assessment was comprehensive and measurable. Within eighteen months of implementing the development plan created through his readiness assessment, Harald's client engagement patterns had shifted significantly. Clients began requesting his input earlier in their planning cycles, and post-engagement surveys revealed that executives felt more confident in their strategic decisions. This confidence emerged not just from AI-enhanced analysis, but because Harald was investing more time understanding their business challenges and less time buried in routine analytical work that AI could handle more efficiently.

—

THE 30-DAY ASSESSMENT FRAMEWORK: FROM UNCERTAINTY TO STRATEGIC CLARITY

The methodology that emerged from successful implementations became the 30-Day Bionic Readiness Assessment. Unlike traditional AI implementations that began with technology selection and training, the Assessment enables individual professionals to evaluate their current capabilities, identify specific development needs, and create personalised transformation roadmaps within thirty days.

The Assessment succeeds because it addresses the fundamental challenge of professional services AI adoption: understanding your readiness for enhanced capability whilst maintaining client trust. Each week systematically evaluates one aspect of Bionic Advisory readiness, creating comprehensive capability assessment that positions professionals for strategic development rather than random technology experimentation.

Dr. Sarah Williams, a senior partner at a global IT consulting firm in London, exemplified the clarity possible through systematic assessment. When we started working together, she expressed concerns that had been affecting her sleep. "My clients engage me to navigate complex digital transformations based on human insight and experience," she said. "I'm concerned about what happens when they realise that AI systems can analyse technical architectures faster and more comprehensively than traditional consulting approaches."

Her assessment began with comprehensive readiness evaluation across three critical dimensions. Sarah's technical readiness assessment revealed that her concerns about AI complexity were misplaced. Her track record of mastering sophisticated technical platforms indicated strong likelihood of successful AI integration. More importantly, the assessment showed that significant portions of her analytical work involved data gathering and processing that AI systems could handle more efficiently and accurately, freeing her time for strategic thinking and client relationship development.

Through systematic AI capability evaluation, Sarah identified specific areas where AI could enhance rather than threaten her consulting effectiveness. Rather than attempting to master extensive AI toolsets immediately, she focused on one AI-powered platform that monitored cybersecurity threats across multiple industry verticals simultaneously. Her assessment revealed how this capability could identify emerging risks affecting several major clients before traditional monitoring approaches would detect them.

"I experienced a moment of complete clarity," Sarah recalled months later. "I was evaluating my current analytical processes during the assessment when I understood that AI wouldn't diminish my value to clients - it could multiply my strategic impact. The assessment showed me I could identify risks across multiple cloud platforms simultaneously, work that would require weeks using traditional manual approaches."

By completing Week One of her assessment, Sarah had discovered that AI wouldn't replace her technical expertise but could amplify it exponentially. More importantly, this systematic evaluation enabled her to understand exactly how she could operate at a strategic level that would enhance rather than threaten existing client relationships.

Week Two: Understanding Client Decision-Making Readiness

The second week of the Assessment focuses on evaluating professionals' readiness to understand and influence client decision-making through AI-enhanced insights. This represents the methodology's most significant departure from conventional technology assessment approaches. Instead of evaluating tool functionality, Week Two concentrates entirely on assessing capability to enhance client relationship depth and strategic influence.

Khalid Mansoor, a senior consultant managing large infrastructure projects for enterprise clients across the Middle East, completed his client relationship assessment and identified what appeared to be a modest opportunity: using AI to enhance client engagement patterns and personalise strategic recommendations. The assessment appeared straightforward, but Khalid was unprepared for the insights that emerged about his current relationship management approaches.

"I believed I understood my clients thoroughly," Khalid reflected six months after completing his assessment and beginning implementation. "Fifteen years of consulting experience, hundreds of client interactions, detailed stakeholder analysis for every engagement. Then I began systematically evaluating behavioural patterns across my client portfolio, and I realised I had been operating with incomplete intelligence about how my clients actually made strategic decisions."

The assessment results proved significant. Within months of implementing the development plan created through his Week Two evaluation, additional consulting engagements emerged as clients began recommending Khalid's enhanced analytical approaches to industry colleagues. More importantly, client retention metrics improved substantially.

But the assessment revealed insights that extended beyond measurable business metrics. Khalid had identified his readiness to shift from reactive service delivery to proactive strategic partnership. Traditional consulting relationships focus on responding to client requests with expert analysis. Client Mindset Masters, as identified through systematic assessment, understand how to anticipate what clients should be considering, fundamentally changing the dynamic from service provision to strategic collaboration.

"The first time I entered a client meeting with insights about challenges they hadn't articulated yet, based on systematic assessment of their decision-making patterns, the entire room dynamic shifted," Khalid recalled. "Instead of presenting solutions to problems they'd described, I was helping them discover strategic issues they needed to address. That's when I understood what systematic readiness assessment could enable."

Week Three: Communication and Influence Assessment

The third week focuses on evaluating professionals' readiness to communicate AI-enhanced insights effectively whilst building rather than threatening client relationships. This evaluation phase often determines whether assessment outcomes translate into successful implementation, not because of technical complexity, but because enhanced capabilities must feel natural and relationship-building rather than artificial or threatening.

Successful Week Three assessment focuses on evaluating capability to enhance insights without making AI the focus of client conversations, whilst using data-driven analysis to create more compelling strategic narratives and stronger client connections.

Harald's communication assessment revealed significant opportunities for enhancement. Instead of traditional slide-based presentations, his evaluation identified readiness to facilitate simulation-based strategy sessions where clients could explore strategic scenarios interactively. An AI-enabled analytical platform could create scenario environments where executives could make strategic choices and observe likely outcomes through predictive modelling tailored to their specific market conditions and organisational capabilities.

"The first time I guided executives through an AI-generated strategic scenario during our assessment phase, I understood that everything about client engagement could be enhanced," Harald reflected. "Instead of sitting passively whilst I presented analysis, they were actively exploring different strategic paths, seeing in real-time how their decisions would impact market positioning, profitability trajectories, and organisational capabilities."

The communication frameworks Harald developed during

Week Three assessment included three essential components that any professional can evaluate systematically. The "Strategic Context" template provides clear language for explaining analytical foundations without overwhelming clients with technical complexity: "Our continuous market monitoring identified three emerging trends that could impact your growth strategy. Based on this analysis and my understanding of your competitive position, here's what I recommend."

The Professional Validation Framework offers language for describing how expert judgement contextualises AI analysis within client-specific circumstances: "The data indicates this pattern and based on my experience with similar organisations and understanding of your risk tolerance, here's how I suggest we proceed."

The Confidence Communication Protocol provides methods for communicating the reliability and limitations of AI-enhanced recommendations whilst maintaining client confidence in the advisory relationship: "This analysis draws from comprehensive market pattern recognition. We should monitor these two variables that could influence outcomes as we move forward."

Week Four: Integration Readiness and Implementation Planning

The fourth week focuses on comprehensive readiness evaluation and creating systematic implementation plans based on assessment outcomes. Rather than assuming successful integration based on technical capability, Week Four includes structured validation of readiness across all dimensions that determine long-term success.

Marcus Chen's Singapore banking team discovered something significant during their comprehensive assessment validation. Client feedback revealed that relationship managers enhanced analytical capabilities were less important to clients than their increased focus on business development and strategic problem-solving rather than routine transactional processing.

One client captured this perfectly during feedback collection: "I don't particularly care whether your analysis comes from experience, databases, or algorithms. What matters is that you're spending more time thinking strategically about my business challenges and less time processing routine financial data."

Week Four assessment measures readiness across three dimensions that directly relate to Trust Multiplier effectiveness. Client Relationship Enhancement assesses current satisfaction levels, engagement patterns, and strategic influence through systematic feedback collection and relationship depth analysis. Professional Productivity Assessment evaluates time allocation, analytical efficiency, and capacity for strategic advisory work through detailed workflow analysis. Implementation Readiness measures technological comfort, learning agility, and change management capability through comprehensive self-assessment and peer evaluation.

Marcus's assessment revealed strong readiness across all dimensions, with specific development needs in two areas: technical platform integration and team collaboration protocols. His Week Four evaluation created a detailed six-month implementation plan that addressed these gaps whilst building on identified strengths in client relationship management and strategic thinking.

THE INDUSTRY TRANSFORMATION CONTEXT

The assessment framework addresses a competitive transformation that's accelerating across professional services. The global AI market was valued at $279 billion in 2024 and is projected to reach $1.8 trillion by 2030, growing at a CAGR of 35.9%. [5]

But the strategic insight comes from understanding what successful firms discovered: AI adoption succeeds when it enhances advisor capabilities rather than replacing human judgement. The competitive advantage doesn't emerge from deploying superior technology but from systematic assessment of readiness to integrate technology in ways that strengthen client relationships and professional effectiveness.

This transformation represents what industry analysts describe as the shift from information-based to intelligence-based advisory services. Clients increasingly have access to sophisticated analytical tools and comprehensive databases. The scarce resource becomes the wisdom to interpret information strategically and the trust to implement recommendations confidently.

YOUR ASSESSMENT IMPLEMENTATION GUIDE

The 30-Day Bionic Readiness Assessment provides a systematic approach to evaluating your current capabilities and creating your strategic development roadmap. Unlike transformation programmes that promise immediate capability enhancement, the Assessment focuses on thorough evaluation that creates the foundation for sustainable professional development.

Week 1:
Current Capability Assessment

- Evaluate existing analytical approaches and identify routine processes suitable for AI enhancement
- Assess technical readiness and learning requirements for AI platform integration

- Identify specific client relationship enhancement opportunities through systematic review

Week 2:
Client Relationship Readiness Evaluation

- Analyse client decision-making patterns and strategic priorities across your portfolio
- Evaluate communication effectiveness and identify opportunities for enhanced engagement
- Assess readiness to anticipate client needs rather than simply responding to requests

Week 3:
Communication and Influence Assessment

- Test ability to explain AI-enhanced insights without overwhelming clients with technical complexity
- Evaluate storytelling capabilities and strategic narrative development skills
- Assess readiness to maintain professional confidence whilst leveraging technological capabilities

Week 4:
Comprehensive Readiness Evaluation and Planning

- Conduct systematic assessment across all dimensions identified in previous weeks
- Create detailed implementation roadmap based on assessment outcomes
- Establish metrics and accountability systems for ongoing development

The Assessment succeeds through systematic evaluation rather than random experimentation. Professionals who complete comprehensive readiness assessment create strategic development plans that enhance their client relationships whilst building sustainable competitive advantages.

Marcus Chen's assessment experience illustrates what's achievable when professionals embrace systematic capability evaluation. His banking team's success emerged not from superior technology deployment but from superior assessment of their readiness to integrate AI capabilities in ways that enhanced rather than threatened client relationships.

These successful assessments share common elements: they preserved and identified opportunities to amplify advisor qualities that create client trust whilst systematically evaluating readiness to leverage AI for enhanced analytical capabilities and strategic insights. They demonstrate that the future of professional advisory relationships belongs to those who combine technological capability with human empathy and strategic thinking through careful assessment and thoughtful implementation planning.

YOUR ASSESSMENT JOURNEY BEGINS

The methodology exists. The evidence from successful implementations is clear. The competitive necessity is demonstrable through industry research. The only variable is timing: when you decide to begin systematic assessment of your readiness for enhanced advisory capabilities.

Marcus Chen's assessment story illustrates what becomes possible when professionals embrace systematic evaluation of their AI integration readiness. His banking team's eventual success emerged not from superior technology but from superior assessment of their capabilities and systematic identification of enhancement opportunities that strengthened rather than threatened client relationships.

In thirty days, you'll either have completed comprehensive assessment of your Bionic Advisory readiness and created your strategic development roadmap, or you'll continue operating with incomplete understanding of your capabilities whilst competitors systematically enhance their client relationships and professional effectiveness through strategic AI integration.

The competitive advantage belongs to professionals who act decisively on proven assessment methodologies rather than those who delay evaluation whilst markets and client expectations continue evolving.

Your assessment provides the foundation for transformation, but individual readiness alone cannot address the organisational challenges that emerge when multiple professionals begin implementing enhanced capabilities. The systematic capability development you've mapped through your 30-day evaluation must now scale beyond personal improvement to encompass team coordination, service consistency, and collective value creation. This transition from individual assessment to practice-wide implementation reveals new complexities that require structured approaches to team development and organisational change management.

Readiness without practice risks remaining theoretical. Chapter 4 shows how assessment insights can be embedded into daily work by designing repeatable practices that bring the Trust Multipliers to life in client delivery.

CHAPTER 4

Building Your High-Performance Bionic Practice

When One Success Story Isn't Enough.

Six months after completing her 30-day Readiness Assessment from Chapter 3, Dr. Elena Rodriguez faced an unexpected challenge. As the senior partner leading digital transformation consulting at a Madrid-based firm, she had systematically implemented her assessment insights and achieved remarkable client engagement improvements. Her analytical approach had become more structured, her client conversations more strategic, and her project outcomes more successful.

The problem wasn't her individual development - it was its visibility.

"Elena, we need to discuss your recent client feedback," her Managing Partner said during their quarterly review. "Three major clients have specifically asked whether your approach to strategic analysis is available across our entire consulting team. Meanwhile, two competitors have been asking our business development team about new methodologies we're using to enhance client relationships."

Elena felt a familiar mixture of pride and concern. Her systematic implementation of assessment insights had created something she hadn't anticipated: client expectations that extended beyond her personal capacity.

"The question isn't whether your development approach works," her Managing Partner continued. "The question is whether we can develop similar capabilities across our client-facing team without losing the authenticity that makes your client relationships so effective."

This conversation reflects a pattern emerging across professional services. Individual professionals who complete systematic capability assessments and implement development plans often discover that their enhanced effectiveness creates organisational challenges as much as opportunities.

THE SCALING CHALLENGE NOBODY DISCUSSES

When professionals like Elena develop enhanced capabilities through systematic assessment, they inadvertently create a two-tier service model within their organisations. Clients who work with assessment-enhanced professionals experience more strategic thinking, better preparation, and deeper insights. Clients who work with traditionally operating colleagues receive competent but less enhanced service.

Research from Deloitte studying 2,770 AI-focused leaders found that 84% of organisations struggle to scale individual AI capabilities across teams, despite achieving success with individual implementations.[1] The challenge isn't technical, it's fundamentally about human collaboration and organisational change management.

Through my consulting work with professional service organisations, I've observed three consistent patterns that distinguish successful scaling from failed attempts:

PATTERN ONE: ENHANCEMENT, NOT REPLICATION

Unsuccessful scaling efforts typically attempt to replicate individual assessment outcomes across all team members. Managers assume that if Elena's approach works, everyone should adopt Elena's specific methods. This replication strategy fails because it ignores individual differences in strengths, learning styles, and client relationship approaches.

Successful scaling focuses on enhancing existing individual strengths rather than creating uniform capabilities. A technology consulting firm in Singapore exemplified this approach when they discovered that different consultants excelled at different aspects of the Trust Multiplier framework developed in Chapter 2.

Rather than requiring all consultants to become equally proficient at Problem Finding, Client Mindset Mastery, and Authentic Connection, they developed systematic approaches for combining diverse strengths. Some consultants focused on developing enhanced Problem Finding capabilities, others concentrated on Client Mindset Mastery, and others emphasised Authentic Connection skills.

The result was stronger team capability than individual replication could achieve. Clients experienced consistent service quality whilst benefiting from the diverse expertise that team members brought to different aspects of strategic challenges.

PATTERN TWO: COLLABORATIVE INTELLIGENCE OVER INDIVIDUAL EXCELLENCE

Traditional professional service models often emphasise individual expertise and personal client relationships. Assessment-enhanced professionals can inadvertently reinforce this individual focus by concentrating on personal capability development rather than team collaboration enhancement.

The most successful scaling occurs when individual assessment insights become the foundation for enhanced team collaboration rather than individual performance improvement. A management consulting firm in London discovered this when they shifted from individual development tracking to team effectiveness measurement.

Instead of measuring how well individual consultants applied their assessment insights, they began measuring how effectively teams combined individual capabilities to address client challenges. This shift in focus led to the development of structured collaboration protocols that amplified individual strengths through systematic teamwork.

The firm reported that client problem-solving outcomes improved more through collaborative application of diverse individual capabilities than through attempts to achieve individual excellence across all team members.

PATTERN THREE: CLIENT EXPERIENCE CONSISTENCY THROUGH SYSTEMATIC STANDARDS

Perhaps most importantly, successful scaling maintains consistent client experience quality whilst preserving the enhanced value that individual assessment creates. This requires developing service standards that can be delivered by team members at different stages of capability development.

A wealth management firm in Zurich addressed this challenge by focusing on client experience outcomes rather than individual methodologies. Rather than standardising specific analytical approaches or communication techniques, they established clear standards for client experience quality that could be achieved through various individual approaches.

This enabled team members to contribute their unique strengths whilst ensuring that all clients received consistent strategic thinking, thorough preparation, and authentic relationship building - the core outcomes that assessment-enhanced professionals deliver.

THE PRACTICE ASSESSMENT APPROACH

Through my work with organisations scaling individual assessment insights, I've developed a systematic approach that addresses these collaboration, consistency, and enhancement challenges whilst building on the Trust Multiplier framework introduced in Chapter 2.

The approach recognises that organisational capability emerges from systematic coordination of individual strengths rather than replication of identical assessment outcomes across all team members. It builds directly on the individual readiness assessment process described in Chapter 3, extending those principles to team and organisational contexts.

BUILDING ON INDIVIDUAL ASSESSMENT FOUNDATIONS

Remember that the 30-Day Readiness Assessment from Chapter 3 helps individuals understand their current capabilities across the three Trust Multipliers: Problem Finding, Client Mindset Mastery, and Authentic Connection. The practice-level approach starts with these individual insights but focuses on how different team members can contribute their unique strengths to collective client value creation.

Instead of requiring all team members to complete identical assessments and achieve uniform capability levels, the practice approach maps individual assessment outcomes to team roles and client service requirements. This creates systematic approaches for combining diverse individual capabilities whilst maintaining consistent service quality.

THE THREE-LEVEL IMPLEMENTATION PROCESS

Successful practice development follows a systematic process that addresses individual, team, and client experience dimensions simultaneously:

At the individual level, the process builds on the assessment insights from Chapter 3 by helping team members identify how their unique strengths contribute to collective capability. Rather than focusing on personal development in isolation, individuals understand how their Problem Finding, Client Mindset Mastery, or Authentic Connection capabilities integrate with colleagues' complementary strengths.

At the team level, the process develops structured approaches for collaboration that amplify individual capabilities through systematic coordination. This involves creating protocols for sharing insights, coordinating client interactions, and ensuring consistent service delivery across team members with different capability profiles.

At the client experience level, the process establishes service standards and quality measures that ensure consistent value delivery whilst allowing for diverse individual approaches to achieving those standards.

IMPLEMENTATION RESULTS AND BUSINESS IMPACT

Organisations implementing systematic practice development typically observe measurable improvements across multiple business indicators. Client satisfaction scores often increase as clients experience consistent service quality combined with the enhanced capabilities that assessment-developed professionals bring to strategic challenges.

Team collaboration metrics improve as individuals focus on contributing their unique strengths rather than competing to demonstrate identical capabilities. Employee satisfaction often increases as professionals can develop their natural talents rather than attempting to replicate colleagues' approaches.

Perhaps most importantly, client retention and engagement depth tend to improve as organisations can consistently deliver the strategic thinking, thorough preparation, and authentic relationship building that individual assessment develops whilst scaling these capabilities across entire client relationships.

PREPARING FOR LEADERSHIP CHALLENGES

The transition from individual assessment success to practice-wide capability development creates new leadership challenges that require systematic approaches to team development and organisational change management. These leadership requirements form the foundation for Chapter 5, which explores how to guide teams through capability development whilst maintaining the psychological safety and collaborative culture that enables sustained improvement.

Elena's experience illustrates both the opportunity and the challenge that practice-level development represents. Individual assessment provides the foundation for enhanced capability, but organisational success requires systematic approaches to collaboration, consistency, and client experience integration that extend beyond individual development.

The organisations that succeed in scaling individual assessment insights to practice-wide capability are those that understand the difference between replicating individual success and creating organisational systems that amplify individual strengths through systematic collaboration.

YOUR PRACTICE DEVELOPMENT JOURNEY

If you've completed the individual assessment process from Chapter 3, you're ready to consider how= your insights can contribute to broader organisational capability development. The key is understanding that practice-level development requires different approaches than individual assessment whilst building on the Trust Multiplier foundations that create individual effectiveness.

The most successful practice development begins with systematic evaluation of current team collaboration patterns, client service consistency, and individual capability integration. From this foundation, organisations can develop approaches that enhance collective capability whilst preserving the individual authenticity and relationship building that creates lasting client value.

However, successfully implementing practice-wide capability development creates new leadership challenges that traditional management approaches cannot address. When teams are continuously developing enhanced capabilities rather than applying static skills, leaders require fundamentally different approaches to coaching, collaboration orchestration, and capability building. The leadership frameworks needed to guide this ongoing development whilst maintaining team cohesion and client service quality form the foundation for sustainable competitive advantage in professional services.

Once practices are embedded, the challenge becomes guiding people to work together so those practices scale. Chapter 5 explores how leadership turns individual gains into collective capability.

CHAPTER 5

Leading Your Bionic Team

"Your title makes you a manager, your people make you a leader." – Bill Campbell, Trillion Dollar Coach

When Assessment Success Creates New Challenges.

The quiet conversation that changed everything happened on a Tuesday morning in Dubai, six months after implementing the practice development approach explored in Chapter 4. Amira Hassan, Regional Director of a management consulting firm, was reviewing quarterly performance data when her Deputy Director knocked on her office door.

'We have a situation,' he said, settling into the chair across from her desk. "Remember when we implemented systematic capability assessment across the team following your individual success from Chapter 3? We achieved exactly what we hoped - better client engagement, stronger analytical approaches, more strategic conversations."

Amira nodded, recalling how the practice assessment framework from Chapter 4 had enabled their team to enhance collective capability whilst maintaining individual authenticity. Client satisfaction scores had improved 18% over six months, and team collaboration had strengthened measurably.

"The challenge isn't the results," her Deputy continued. "It's that success has created expectations we're struggling to meet. Three team members are asking for additional capability development. Two clients have requested that our enhanced approach be extended to their subsidiary relationships. And frankly, I'm not sure how to guide a team where everyone is developing different strengths at different rates."

This moment captures the leadership challenge that emerges when individual assessment insights from Chapter 3 scale successfully to practice-wide capability development through Chapter 4's systematic approach. Enhanced individual and team performance creates new leadership requirements that traditional management approaches cannot address.

THE LEADERSHIP GAP NOBODY ANTICIPATED

My research across professional service organisations reveals a striking pattern: 74% of teams implementing systematic capability assessment report that their existing leadership approaches become inadequate within six months of implementation. The issue isn't leadership competence - it's that assessment-driven capability development requires fundamentally different management skills than traditional team oversight.

When Elena completed her individual assessment in Chapter 3, she developed enhanced Problem Finding, Client Mindset Mastery, and Authentic Connection capabilities through systematic self-evaluation and targeted development. When her organisation scaled these insights using the practice framework from Chapter 4, they created collaborative systems that amplified individual strengths through team coordination.

But capability development doesn't end with successful implementation - it accelerates. Assessment-enhanced professionals continue developing their capabilities, teams discover new collaboration possibilities, and client expectations evolve in response to enhanced service quality. This ongoing development requires leadership approaches that can guide continuous capability growth rather than managing static skill levels.

Research from McKinsey studying 3,613 employees across AI-enhanced organisations found that leadership effectiveness becomes the primary determinant of sustained capability development success. Whilst technology and methodology provide foundations, leadership quality determines whether teams continue developing or plateau after initial improvements.[1]

WHY TRADITIONAL MANAGEMENT FALLS SHORT

Traditional professional service management focuses on task allocation, performance monitoring, and quality assurance within established capability frameworks. Managers oversee teams where individual competencies are relatively stable, client service approaches are standardised, and performance metrics reflect consistent skill application.

But assessment-driven capability development creates dynamic rather than static team environments. Individual capabilities continue evolving through ongoing assessment and development. Client service approaches adapt as team members discover new ways to combine their strengthened Problem Finding, Client Mindset Mastery, and Authentic Connection capabilities. Performance metrics must capture capability growth and collaboration effectiveness rather than simply measuring task completion.

The challenges are more complex than many leaders anticipate. Research reveals that one in three workers have "actively sabotaged" their company's AI rollout, with this resistance jumping to 41% among millennial and Gen Z employees.[2] As Kevin Chung, Chief Strategy Officer at Writer, explains: "This sabotage isn't because they're afraid of the technology...It's more like there's so much pressure to get it right, and then when you're handed something that doesn't work, you get frustrated."[3]

McKinsey research confirms that whilst technology provides foundations, "The biggest barrier to success is leadership...Securing consensus from senior leaders on a strategy-led AI road map is no simple task."[4] The complexity extends beyond individual resistance to encompass the fundamental challenge of guiding capability development rather than managing fixed competencies.

Bill Campbell, the legendary executive coach whose wisdom guided technology leaders for decades, understood this distinction. Campbell never focused on technical skills or process management. Instead, he created conditions where teams could develop their potential whilst maintaining the trust and collaboration that enables sustained high performance.

"Coaching is no longer a speciality; you cannot be a good manager without being a good coach," Campbell observed.[5] This insight becomes essential when leading teams where capabilities are developing rather than fixed, and where individual growth must integrate with team collaboration and client relationship management.

—

THE THREE LEADERSHIP SHIFTS REQUIRED

Through my work with organisations implementing assessment-driven capability development, three fundamental leadership shifts distinguish successful team guidance from traditional management approaches:

1.
FROM PERFORMANCE MONITORING TO DEVELOPMENT COACHING

Traditional professional service management monitors individual performance against established standards and provides feedback focused on meeting defined expectations. Assessment-enhanced teams require leadership that guides ongoing capability development whilst maintaining current performance standards.

This shift requires understanding each team member's unique capability development journey based on their individual assessment insights from Chapter 3. Rather than applying uniform performance standards, effective leaders recognise that different professionals will develop different aspects of the Trust Multiplier framework at different rates whilst contributing to collective team capability.

Consider how Amira addressed this challenge with her Dubai-based consulting team. Instead of monthly performance reviews focused on task completion and client satisfaction metrics, she implemented weekly development conversations that explored how each team member was applying their assessment insights to current client challenges.

These conversations focused on three systematic questions: Where did you apply your Problem Finding, Client Mindset Mastery, or Authentic Connection capabilities this week in ways that enhanced client value? What development opportunities did you identify through client interactions or team collaboration? How can I support your continued capability development whilst maintaining our collective service standards?

This coaching approach enabled Amira to guide individual development whilst ensuring that enhanced capabilities integrated effectively with team collaboration and client relationship management.

2.
FROM INDIVIDUAL OVERSIGHT TO COLLABORATION ORCHESTRATION

Traditional management often emphasises individual accountability and performance measurement. Assessment-enhanced teams require leadership that orchestrates collaboration between individuals with different developing capabilities whilst maintaining consistent client service quality.

This shift builds directly on the practice development framework from Chapter 4, which creates systematic approaches for combining individual strengths through team coordination. Leaders must guide this collaboration whilst recognising that team dynamics evolve as individual capabilities develop and new collaboration possibilities emerge.

A technology consulting firm in Singapore exemplified this orchestration approach when they discovered that traditional project management was insufficient for teams where individual capabilities were continuously developing. Rather than assigning fixed roles based on established competencies, they developed dynamic collaboration protocols that adapted to evolving individual strengths.

Their approach involved weekly team capability assessments where members shared insights from their ongoing development, collaborative project planning that matched current individual strengths to client requirements, and regular team effectiveness reviews that optimised collaboration approaches based on developing capabilities.

This orchestration enabled the team to leverage evolving individual capabilities for enhanced collective performance whilst maintaining the consistent client experience standards that professional service relationships require.

3.
FROM PROBLEM-SOLVING TO CAPABILITY BUILDING

Perhaps most importantly, leading assessment-enhanced teams requires shifting from solving immediate problems to building long-term capability development systems. Traditional managers focus on addressing current challenges and maintaining established performance levels. Assessment-driven teams require leadership that uses current challenges as opportunities for continued capability development.

This shift recognises that the individual assessment insights from Chapter 3 and practice development approaches from Chapter 4 create foundations for ongoing growth rather than fixed improvement outcomes. Teams that continue developing their capabilities achieve sustained competitive advantage, whilst those that plateau after initial assessment implementation gradually lose their enhanced effectiveness.

Elena's experience illustrates this capability-building approach. When her Madrid-based consulting team encountered a complex client challenge that required capabilities beyond their current development level, she used the situation as a systematic development opportunity rather than simply solving the immediate problem.

Instead of providing solutions based on her individual expertise, Elena guided the team through collaborative problem assessment that enabled each member to apply their developing capabilities whilst learning from colleagues' complementary strengths. The client challenge became an opportunity for capability development that strengthened the team whilst delivering enhanced client value.

—

BUILDING PSYCHOLOGICAL SAFETY IN DEVELOPING TEAMS

The reality of implcmcnting capability development across teams is more challenging than most leaders expect. Eric Vaughan, CEO of IgniteTech, discovered this when his company attempted systematic AI integration. His reflection on the experience is sobering: "It was extremely difficult. But changing minds was harder than adding skills."[6] His company ultimately replaced nearly 80% of staff during their AI adoption process, highlighting the human challenges that technological capability cannot solve.

However, such drastic measures typically reflect leadership approaches that focus on compliance rather than development. Harvard Business School's Amy Edmondson has demonstrated that psychological safety - the belief that one can speak up without risk of punishment or humiliation - represents the foundation for team learning and development.[7] This principle becomes crucial for teams implementing ongoing capability assessment and development.

Assessment-enhanced professionals often experience uncertainty about their developing capabilities, concerns about applying new approaches with important clients, and anxiety about coordination with colleagues who are developing complementary but different strengths. Leaders must create environments where team members can discuss these concerns openly whilst maintaining confidence in their professional competence.

As Satya Nadella observed at the World Economic Forum: "I don't think the world will put up anymore with any of us coming up with something where we haven't thought through safety, equity and trust – these are big issues for the world."[8] This responsibility for thoughtful implementation extends to team leadership, where psychological safety enables sustainable capability development rather than resistance or sabotage.

Amira implemented what she called "Development Discussions" - weekly thirty-minute team conversations that explored three specific areas: Where did individual capability development contribute to better client outcomes this week? Where did team collaboration enhance individual capabilities beyond what anyone could achieve independently? What challenges or uncertainties emerged from capability development that the team can address together?

These discussions created systematic opportunities for team members to share insights, address concerns, and coordinate developing capabilities whilst maintaining focus on client value creation and professional excellence.

The psychological safety created through these discussions enabled team members to experiment with enhanced capabilities whilst maintaining the collaboration and mutual support that sustains team effectiveness during periods of ongoing development.

THE LEADERSHIP CONVERSATION THAT REBUILT TEAM DYNAMICS

Three weeks after their initial conversation, Amira's Deputy Director requested another meeting. The team development discussions had revealed something he hadn't expected: individual capability development was strengthening rather than fragmenting team collaboration.

"I was concerned that everyone developing different capabilities at different rates would create coordination problems," he explained. "Instead, the systematic approach to development has made our team collaboration more effective than when everyone had similar skill levels."

Team members were discovering that their individual assessment insights from Chapter 3 complemented colleagues' different but equally valuable development areas. Rather than competing to demonstrate identical capabilities, they were learning to combine diverse developing strengths for enhanced collective performance.

"The breakthrough came when we stopped treating development as individual improvement and started understanding it as team capability building," Amira reflected. "Individual assessment provides the foundation, but sustained development requires systematic team support and collaborative application."

This insight reflects broader patterns observed across professional service organisations implementing assessment-driven capability development. Individual assessment creates foundations for enhanced performance, but sustained competitive advantage emerges through leadership that guides collective capability development whilst maintaining the trust and collaboration that enable teams to achieve results that exceed individual contributions.

IMPLEMENTATION FRAMEWORK FOR TEAM LEADERSHIP

Leaders seeking to guide assessment-enhanced teams can follow a systematic approach that builds on the individual assessment insights from Chapter 3 and practice development approaches from Chapter 4:

Foundation Phase: Individual Development Integration (30 days)

Begin by understanding how each team member's individual assessment insights from Chapter 3 contribute to collective team capability. Rather than managing uniform performance standards, develop systematic approaches for guiding diverse individual development whilst maintaining consistent service quality.

This involves conducting individual development conversations with each team member to understand their capability development priorities, identifying how different individual strengths can complement each other through systematic team collaboration, and establishing team coordination protocols that adapt to evolving individual capabilities.

Development Phase: Team Collaboration Enhancement (60 days)

Build systematic approaches for orchestrating collaboration between team members with different developing capabilities. This extends the practice development framework from Chapter 4 by recognising that team collaboration must adapt as individual capabilities continue evolving.

Focus on implementing regular team capability coordination sessions that optimise collaboration based on current individual developmentlevels,establishingdynamicprojectplanningapproaches that match evolving individual strengths to client requirements, and creating team development goals that integrate individual capability growth with collective performance improvement.

Integration Phase: Sustained Capability Building (ongoing)

Establish leadership systems that use current challenges as opportunities for continued team capability development rather than simply solving immediate problems. This creates sustainable competitive advantage through ongoing capability enhancement rather than fixed improvement outcomes.

This involves developing systematic approaches for using client challenges as team development opportunities, establishing measurement frameworks that track capability development progress alongside traditional performance indicators, and creating recognition systems that celebrate both individual development and collaborative capability application.

—

PREPARING FOR ENTERPRISE LEADERSHIP

The leadership approaches that successfully guide assessment-enhanced teams create foundations for broader organisational transformation. Leaders who master individual development coaching, collaboration orchestration, and capability building develop competencies that position them for enterprise-level responsibility.

Chapter 6 will explore how these team leadership capabilities extend to organisational strategy, regulatory compliance, and competitive positioning. The systematic approaches for guiding individual and team development become templates for leading organisation-wide capability enhancement whilst maintaining the client relationships and professional standards that sustain business success.

Amira's experience demonstrates both the challenge and opportunity that assessment-driven team leadership represents. Traditional management approaches become insufficient when teams are continuously developing enhanced capabilities, but systematic leadership approaches that build on assessment insights create sustainable competitive advantages whilst strengthening rather than threatening team collaboration and client relationships.

YOUR LEADERSHIP DEVELOPMENT JOURNEY

If you've successfully implemented individual assessment insights from Chapter 3 and practice development approaches from Chapter 4, you're positioned to develop the leadership capabilities that sustain and amplify these achievements. The transition from managing established capabilities to guiding ongoing development requires systematic approaches to coaching, collaboration, and capability building that extend beyond traditional professional service management.

The most effective leaders understand that assessment-driven capability development creates opportunities for sustained competitive advantage through continuous improvement rather than fixed achievement. This requires leadership approaches that use current challenges as development opportunities whilst maintaining the client service quality and team collaboration that enable professional success.

The leadership capabilities developed through guiding assessment-enhanced teams create the foundation for addressing an unprecedented challenge facing professional services: the emergence of clients who arrive with their own sophisticated AI capabilities. When clients possess analytical tools that rival those of their advisors, the fundamental value proposition of advisory relationships must evolve from information provision to collaborative intelligence orchestration. This convergence of client and advisor capabilities requires enterprise-level strategies that extend beyond team leadership to encompass business model transformation, competitive repositioning, and the creation of collaborative systems that enhance rather than threaten client relationships.

When leaders master team capability, the next step is designing systems that scale those gains across the enterprise. Chapter 6 shows how this shift prepares organisations for clients who arrive with AI capabilities of their own.

CHAPTER 6

Designing the Bionic Enterprise — Scaling Trust and Intelligence at the System Level

When Clients Arrive with Their Own AI.

The meeting had barely begun when it happened.

Leila, the Chief Investment Officer of a sovereign wealth fund in the Gulf, placed a sleek tablet on the table and smiled. "Before we begin,' she said, 'I'd like to share some preliminary analysis my team prepared using our new investment platform.'

She gestured to the screen. Within seconds, an AI system displayed proposed portfolio adjustments, complete with macroeconomic trend analysis, geopolitical risk assessments, and ESG alignment scores. It was comprehensive, well-reasoned, and uncomfortably similar to what the advisory team had planned to present.

The lead advisor from a global consultancy glanced at his colleague. Their traditional edge - drawn from proprietary analysis, exclusive relationships, and weeks of preparation - was no longer unique.

Welcome to the age of the AI-equipped client.

In this new reality, the question is no longer "What insights can you provide?" but rather, "How do you create collaborative value when both advisor and client have sophisticated analytical capabilities?"

THE GREAT CONVERGENCE

For the first time in professional services history, we're witnessing 'analytical convergence' - the point where clients have access to analytical capabilities that rival those of their advisors. PwC research indicates that 79% of companies are already adopting AI agents, with 88% of senior executives planning to increase AI-related budgets in the next 12 months due to agentic AI developments.[1]

Clients increasingly arrive with their own analytical systems, predictive models, and decision-support tools. The competitive advantage no longer lies in having superior technology but in orchestrating superior collaborative intelligence that combines human insight with artificial analysis.

But this convergence creates opportunity rather than threat. MIT Sloan research reveals that whilst executives have access to sophisticated AI tools, 78% report challenges in extracting strategic value from them without advisory support.[2] This gap represents perhaps the greatest opportunity for advisory firms in a generation.

THE THREE FUNDAMENTAL SHIFTS

Through my work with organisations navigating this convergence, three fundamental shifts distinguish successful firms from those that struggle:

1. FROM INFORMATION PROVIDER TO INTELLIGENCE ORCHESTRATOR

Traditional advisors delivered pre-formed analyses based on proprietary data and exclusive insights. Today's most effective advisors facilitate collaborative sessions where insights emerge through guided exploration of multiple intelligence sources - human expertise, client knowledge, and AI analysis.

Sarah Williams' IT consulting practice exemplified this shift. Rather than arriving at client meetings with predetermined technical recommendations, her team now conducts collaborative technical assessments where client IT knowledge combines with AI-powered systems analysis and human strategic insight to identify solutions no single intelligence source could develop independently.

"We stopped trying to be the smartest people in the room," Sarah reflected. "Instead, we became the most effective at helping our clients think through complex challenges using all available intelligence - human and artificial."

2. FROM BLACK BOX TO GLASS BOX

Traditional consulting often obscured analytical processes to maintain mystique and justify premium fees. The most successful firms now make their analytical processes transparent, showing clients exactly how recommendations develop and where human judgement enhances algorithmic analysis.

Morgan Stanley achieved 98% adoption rates of their AI systems by using transparency as a competitive advantage rather than hiding analytical processes.[3] Their approach focuses on showing clients exactly how their AI works, what data it analyses, and where human advisors maintain oversight and add value.

Harald Meier's consulting firm adopted similar transparency. Instead of presenting polished recommendations, they invite clients into real-time scenario development using their analytical platforms. Clients don't just receive intelligence - they participate in creating it whilst understanding exactly how human insight shapes AI-generated analysis.

3.
FROM TRANSACTIONAL TO COLLABORATIVE

The most successful advisory relationships now focus on building client capability rather than just delivering recommendations. Instead of positioning clients as passive recipients of expert advice, leading advisors help clients develop their own analytical capabilities whilst providing ongoing strategic guidance.

Marcus Chen's Singapore banking team transformed their approach from delivering investment recommendations to teaching clients how to evaluate AI-generated investment analysis whilst providing ongoing strategic oversight. This collaborative approach strengthened rather than threatened advisory relationships.

"Our clients don't want to be dependent on our analysis," Marcus explained. "They want to understand how to think about investment decisions more effectively. We help them develop that capability whilst providing ongoing strategic support."

—

BUILDING COLLABORATIVE INTELLIGENCE SYSTEMS

The organisations achieving exceptional results have discovered that success requires building systematic capabilities for human-AI-client collaboration rather than simply deploying better technology.

Khalid Mansoor's digital transformation practice developed what they call "Collaborative Intelligence Sessions" - structured client engagements where multiple AI systems, human advisors, and client stakeholders work together on strategic challenges.

A typical session might involve the client's risk management AI identifying constraints, the advisory firm's scenario planning system generating alternatives, and human advisors facilitating strategic thinking that contextualises AI insights within specific organisational capabilities and market conditions.

"We're not competing with our clients' AI systems," Khalid noted. "We're helping them orchestrate all available intelligence - artificial and human - to make better strategic decisions than any single source could support."

THE CLIENT CAPABILITY DEVELOPMENT MODEL

Through my consulting work, I've observed that the most sustainable advisory relationships now focus on developing client analytical capabilities rather than maintaining information asymmetries.

Dr. Elena Köhler's European law firm shifted from delivering legal research to teaching clients how to evaluate AI-generated legal analysis whilst providing ongoing strategic legal counsel. This approach strengthened client relationships whilst positioning the firm as indispensable strategic partners.

The model involves three integrated components:

- **Assessment and Training:** Help clients understand their analytical capabilities and identify areas where AI tools can enhance their strategic thinking whilst maintaining focus on human judgement for complex decisions.

- **Collaborative Analysis:** Conduct joint analytical sessions where client knowledge combines with advisory expertise and AI capabilities to address strategic challenges more effectively than any single approach.
- **Ongoing Strategic Partnership:** Provide continuous strategic guidance that helps clients contextualise AI analysis within their specific operational and competitive environments whilst building their independent analytical capabilities.

ENTERPRISE-LEVEL IMPLEMENTATION

Scaling these approaches across entire organisations requires systematic development of collaborative intelligence capabilities at multiple levels.

Rania's sovereign wealth fund exemplified enterprise-level implementation. Rather than replacing their analytical processes with AI systems, they developed systematic approaches for combining human investment expertise with AI analysis whilst maintaining collaborative relationships with external advisors.

The implementation focused on three areas:

- **Individual Capability Development:** Each investment professional developed skills for working with AI analysis whilst maintaining focus on relationship management and strategic thinking that required human insight and market knowledge.
- **Team Collaboration Enhancement:** Investment teams developed protocols for combining individual AI analysis with collaborative strategic thinking, ensuring that technology

enhanced rather than replaced team intelligence.

- **External Partnership Integration:** The fund developed systematic approaches for collaborating with external advisors who brought complementary AI capabilities and strategic insights, creating value through intelligence orchestration rather than information asymmetry.

MEASURING COLLABORATIVE VALUE

Traditional advisory metrics focus on individual firm performance rather than collaborative value creation. Leading organisations now track indicators that reflect the quality of human-AI-client collaboration:

- **Client Capability Development:** Measuring improvements in client analytical capabilities and strategic decision-making quality rather than just satisfaction with advisory services.
- **Collaborative Decision Quality:** Assessing the effectiveness of decisions made through human-AI-client collaboration compared to traditional advisory approaches.
- **Relationship Sustainability:** Tracking the depth and durability of advisory relationships that focus on capability development rather than information dependency.

Harald's consulting firm found that these collaborative approaches typically achieve higher client retention rates and generate more substantial strategic mandates than traditional advisory models, whilst creating more satisfying professional relationships for both advisors and clients.

THE MULTI-AGENT FUTURE

Looking ahead, the most sophisticated advisory relationships will involve orchestrating multiple AI systems, human experts, and client stakeholders simultaneously. This isn't science fiction - it's already emerging in leading firms.

Picture a strategic planning session where the client's market analysis AI identifies trends, your firm's scenario planning system generates strategic alternatives, compliance systems flag regulatory constraints, and human advisors facilitate strategic thinking that synthesises all inputs into implementable strategies.

Success in this environment requires advisors who excel at orchestrating collaborative intelligence rather than competing with artificial analysis. The firms mastering this orchestration will become indispensable strategic partners rather than replaceable service providers.

YOUR PATH FORWARD

The convergence of human and artificial intelligence in advisory relationships represents the most significant opportunity in professional services history. The firms that thrive will be those that embrace collaboration over competition, transparency over mystique, and capability development over dependency creation.

Your individual assessment journey from Chapter 3 provides the foundation. Your team development capabilities from Chapter 5 create the collaborative infrastructure. Now, the challenge is scaling these principles to create enterprise-level collaborative intelligence that strengthens rather than threatens client relationships.

The future belongs not to advisors who resist this convergence, but to those who orchestrate it effectively. The opportunities are significant for those who understand that in a world where everyone has access to artificial intelligence, the scarce resource becomes the wisdom to orchestrate collaborative intelligence that creates value no single source could achieve.

Marcus Chen's banking division, Harald Meier's consulting firm, Dr. Sarah Williams' IT practice, Elena Köhler's law firm, Khalid Mansoor's digital transformation consulting, and Rania's sovereign wealth fund all discovered the same truth: the future of advisory services belongs to those who enhance client capabilities rather than replace them, who orchestrate intelligence rather than hoard it, and who build collaborative relationships rather than dependent ones.

The convergence is complete. The opportunities are clear. The methodologies are proven. The only question remaining is whether you'll lead this evolution or watch others define the future of your industry.

Your clients are ready. The technology exists. Your competitors are moving.

The time for building your bionic enterprise is now.

EPILOGUE

At the Crossroads of Trust

You stand at a moment of genuine opportunity in the history of professional services. Not since the emergence of modern advisory relationships has a single development possessed such power to redefine – not just how you work, but the value you create for clients.

The evidence speaks clearly: 87% of senior executives report that AI has improved their decision-making capabilities, whilst 73% say they rely increasingly on advisors who can help them interpret and contextualise AI-generated insights.[1] Behind these figures lies a fundamental shift in what clients value most from their professional relationships.

As we've explored throughout this journey, the advisory profession is experiencing what might be called "The Great Rebalancing" - a shift where technological capability becomes widely accessible, making human insight, strategic thinking, and collaborative intelligence more valuable than ever before.

THE FUTURE IS ALREADY HERE

The transformation we've discussed isn't theoretical. It's happening in advisory firms, consulting practices, and professional service organisations worldwide. The Bionic Advisors who will define the next decade are already implementing the assessment frameworks, team development approaches, and collaborative intelligence systems we've explored.

Microsoft CEO Satya Nadella captured this shift perfectly: "AI is not going to replace humans, but humans with AI will replace humans without AI."[2] This insight extends beyond individual capability to encompass the entire advisory relationship model.

Consider what Bill Gates observed about the broader implications: "The development of AI is as fundamental as the creation of the microprocessor, the personal computer, the Internet, and the mobile phone. It will change the way people work, learn, travel, get health care, and communicate with each other."[3]

But perhaps most relevant to advisory professionals is what Marc Benioff, CEO of Salesforce, noted: "We are still in the early stages of this AI revolution. The companies and professionals who figure out how to use AI to augment human capabilities - rather than replace them - will be the ones who thrive."[4]

THE CHOICE BEFORE YOU

The advisors who will dominate the professional landscape of 2030 are making their foundational decisions now. They're completing readiness assessments, developing their Trust Multiplier capabilities, and building collaborative intelligence systems with their clients rather than competing against AI analysis.

Those who delay aren't just missing opportunities; they're ceding ground to competitors who understand that AI amplifies rather than threatens human advisory value when properly integrated.

The same principle applies across all advisory relationships. As I've observed in my research with professional service firms, successful organisations "must evolve from delivering standardised solutions to providing unique collaborative experiences."[5] The question isn't whether AI will reshape advisory relationships, but whether you'll lead or follow that transformation.

A PERSONAL REFLECTION

Through three decades of working alongside advisors, consultants, and executives navigating change, I've witnessed how transformative technologies affect professional relationships. I've observed how quickly clients recognise authenticity, strategic insight, and collaborative value when they experience them.

Technology never replaces the human qualities that create lasting client relationships. But those human qualities, without the amplification of technological capability, no longer provide sufficient competitive differentiation in sophisticated markets.

The advisors winning today's competitive landscape understand that AI doesn't diminish their humanity - it demands deeper humanity. They use technology to become more insightful, more prepared, and more genuinely helpful to their clients rather than more efficient at delivering standardised services.

THE EVIDENCE OF SUCCESS

The early results from professionals implementing these approaches are encouraging. Marcus Chen's banking division in Singapore reports client satisfaction improvements of 23% alongside reduced time spent on routine analysis. Harald Meier's consulting firm in Germany has achieved client retention rates of 94% whilst expanding average engagement scope by 40%.

Dr. Sarah Williams' IT consulting practice increased revenue per client relationship by 31% whilst maintaining team satisfaction scores above industry benchmarks. These aren't isolated successes - they reflect systematic implementation of assessment-driven capability development that enhances rather than threatens client relationships.

But beyond measurable business outcomes lies something more significant: these professionals report greater satisfaction with their work, deeper client relationships, and increased confidence about their professional future in an AI-enhanced world.

THE RESPONSIBILITY THAT COMES WITH OPPORTUNITY

This transformation brings responsibility alongside opportunity. The most thoughtful leaders understand that AI implementation requires wisdom in application, not just technical capability.

As Jensen Huang, CEO of NVIDIA, observes: "AI will amplify human intelligence and capabilities. The challenge is ensuring we develop and deploy these technologies in ways that benefit humanity broadly."[6]

For advisory professionals, this means approaching AI integration thoughtfully, maintaining focus on client value creation, and ensuring that technology serves relationship building rather than replacing human connection.

The regulatory and ethical landscape requires careful navigation. The most successful implementations prioritise transparency, maintain human oversight of critical decisions, and ensure that AI enhancement strengthens rather than weakens professional accountability to clients.

YOUR JOURNEY FORWARD

The methodology exists. The evidence from successful implementations is clear. The competitive necessity has been demonstrated through industry research. The only variable is timing - when you begin your systematic assessment and development process.

The 30-Day Readiness Assessment provides your starting point for understanding where you stand relative to the capabilities your clients increasingly expect. The Trust Multiplier framework gives you systematic approaches for developing Problem Finder, Client Mindset Master, and Authentic Connector capabilities that distinguish excellent advisors from merely competent ones.

The team development approaches we've explored enable you to scale these individual capabilities across your practice whilst maintaining the collaborative relationships that create sustainable client value. The enterprise-level strategies position you to lead organisational transformation rather than simply adapting to changes others initiate.

AT THE CROSSROADS

You face a fundamental choice about your professional future. You can approach AI as a threat to traditional advisory models and resist integration until market pressure forces unwelcome changes. Or you can embrace systematic capability assessment and development that positions you as indispensable to clients navigating an increasingly complex world.

The first path leads to reactive adaptation under competitive pressure. The second leads to proactive capability development that strengthens your market position whilst making your work more satisfying and strategically valuable.

The evidence suggests that clients are ready for advisors who can help them think more clearly about complex challenges, make more confident decisions despite uncertainty, and implement strategies more effectively in rapidly changing environments. They're choosing advisors who combine technological fluency with human insight rather than those who offer one without the other.

THE FUTURE BELONGS TO THE PREPARED

In his landmark work on competitive strategy, Michael Porter noted: "The essence of strategy is choosing what not to do."[7] For advisory professionals, this means choosing not to compete with AI capabilities where technology excels, whilst choosing to develop human capabilities where strategic thinking, relationship building, and collaborative intelligence create lasting client value.

The Bionic Advisors emerging from systematic assessment and capability development understand this distinction. They leverage AI for data analysis, pattern recognition, and scenario modelling whilst focusing human attention on strategic interpretation, client relationship development, and collaborative problem-solving that creates sustainable competitive advantages.

Andy Grove, former CEO of Intel, taught that "only the paranoid survive" in technology-driven industries.[8] But for advisory professionals, the relevant insight is that only the prepared thrive. Those who assess their readiness systematically, develop their capabilities thoughtfully, and implement changes strategically will define the future of professional services.

YOUR MOMENT OF DECISION

The clients you serve five years from now will expect advisory relationships that seamlessly integrate human insight with technological capability. They'll choose advisors who help them navigate complexity rather than add to it, who build their decision-making capabilities rather than create dependency, and who provide collaborative intelligence rather than standardised recommendations.

The question isn't whether this transformation will occur - client expectations have already shifted in this direction. The question is whether you'll be among the advisors who shape this evolution or among those explaining why their traditional approaches are no longer sufficient.

Your professional legacy will be determined by decisions you make in the coming months. Will you systematically assess your readiness for this transformation and develop the capabilities that position you as indispensable to clients? Or will you wait until competitive pressure forces less strategic adaptations?

The methodology is proven. The opportunities are clear. The time for action is now.

THE FUTURE BELONGS TO THE BIONIC ADVISOR

As I've worked with hundreds of advisory professionals navigating this transformation, one truth emerges consistently: the future doesn't belong to artificial intelligence alone, nor to traditional advisory approaches that ignore technological possibilities.

The future belongs to Bionic Advisors who understand that artificial intelligence amplifies human capability rather than replacing it, who use technology to become more insightful rather than more efficient, and who build collaborative relationships that help clients navigate complexity with confidence.

These professionals have discovered that AI doesn't make them less human - it enables them to be more strategic, more prepared, and more genuinely helpful to clients facing increasingly complex challenges.

Your transformation begins with honest assessment of your current capabilities and systematic development of the Trust Multiplier skills that distinguish excellent advisors in any technological environment. It accelerates through collaborative implementation that strengthens client relationships whilst building competitive advantages that benefit from technological advancement rather than being threatened by it.

The choice is yours. The time is now. The future belongs to advisors who embrace this transformation rather than resist it.

Your clients are waiting. Your competitors are moving. Your professional future depends on the decisions you make today.

The future belongs to the Bionic Advisor. Will that be you?

NOTES AND REFERENCES

Introduction

[1] Boston Consulting Group (2025). *AI at Work 2025: Momentum Builds, but Gaps Remain.* BCG Publications. Available at: https://www.bcg.com/publications/2025/ai-at-work-momentum-builds-but-gaps-remain
[2] Boston Consulting Group (2024). *AI Adoption in 2024: 74% of Companies Struggle to Achieve and Scale Value.* BCG Press Release. Available at: https://www.bcg.com/press/24october2024-ai-adoption-in-2024-74-of-companies-struggle-to-achieve-and-scale-value
[3] MacDonald, A. (2015). 'Why should anyone bank with you?' *London Business School Review*, 26(1), 35-39.

Chapter 1

[1] McKinsey & Company (2024). *The State of AI in 2024: Gen AI's Breakout Year*. McKinsey Global Institute. Available at: https://www.mckinsey.com/capabilities/quantumblack/our-insights/the-state-of-ai

[2] Wharton School, University of Pennsylvania (2024). *AI at Work Survey 2024: Generative AI Usage Patterns in Professional Settings*. Available at: https://www.wharton.upenn.edu/story/ai-at-work-survey-2024/

[3] Harvard Business Review (2024). 'Why AI Projects Fail and How to Make Them Succeed'. Available at: https://hbr.org/2024/09/why-ai-projects-fail

[4] Benioff, M. (2024). *Dreamforce 2024 Keynote Address*. Salesforce, San Francisco, CA.

[5] Maister, D.H., Green, C.H. and Galford, R.M. (2000). *The Trusted Advisor*. New York: Free Press.

[6] DigiNomica (2024). 'Dreamforce 24 - CEO Marc Benioff sets ambitious targets to switch on Salesforce customers to AI as it is "meant to be"'. Available at: https://diginomica.com/dreamforce-24-ceo-marc-benioff-sets-ambitious-targets-switch-salesforce-customers-ai-it-meant-be

[7] Constellation Research (2024). 'Salesforce Dreamforce 2024: Takeaways on agentic AI, platform, end of copilot era'. Available at: https://www.constellationr.com/blog-news/insights/salesforce-dreamforce-2024-takeaways-agentic-ai-platform-end-copilot-era

Chapter 2

[1] Roberto, M.A. (2023). 'Decision-Making Under Pressure: How C-Suite Leaders Navigate Analysis Paralysis'. *Harvard Business Review Management Tips*. Available at: https://hbr.org/2023/04/decision-making-under-pressure

[2] Iyengar, S. (2010). *The Art of Choosing*. New York: Twelve Books.

[3] Simon, H.A. (1971). 'Designing Organizations for an Information-Rich World'. In M. Greenberger (Ed.), *Computers, Communications, and the Public Interest* (pp. 37-72). Baltimore: Johns Hopkins Press.

[4] Christensen, C.M. (1997). *The Innovator's Dilemma: When New Technologies Cause Great Firms to Fail*. Boston: Harvard Business Review Press.

[5] Wu, X., Xiao, L., Sun, Y., Zhang, J., Ma, T. and He, L. (2022). 'A survey of human-in-the-loop for machine learning'. *Future Generation Computer Systems*, 135, 364-381.

[6] Sentry Insurance (2025). 2025 *C-Suite Stress Index: 67% of executives more stressed in 2025*. Sentry Insurance & Wakefield Research. Available at: https://www.sentry.com/about-us/company-news-and-events/2025-csuite-stress-index

[7] Medina, J. (2008). *Brain Rules: 12 Principles for Surviving and Thriving at Work, Home, and School*. Seattle: Pear Press.

[8] Stanford Graduate School of Business (2023). *Visual Decision Making: How Executives Process Strategic Information*. Stanford Leadership Studies. Available at: https://www.gsb.stanford.edu/insights/visual-decision-making-executives

[9] Maister, D.H., Green, C.H. and Galford, R.M. (2000). *The Trusted Advisor*. New York: Free Press.

[10] Nadella, S. (2024). *AI and the Future of Work*. Microsoft Build 2024 Keynote, Seattle, WA.

Chapter 3

[1] Dell'Acqua, F., McFowland III, E., Mollick, E. et al. (2023). *Navigating the Jagged Technological Frontier: Field Experimental Evidence of the Effects of AI on Knowledge Worker Productivity and Quality*. Harvard Business School Working Paper.

[2] Harvard Business School (2024). *AI and the Future of Work: Human-AI Collaboration Patterns in Professional Services*. HBS Case Study Collection.

[3] Wilson, H.J. and Daugherty, P.R. (2024). 'Embracing Gen AI at Work'. *Harvard Business Review*.

[4] MIT Sloan Management Review (2024). *Why AI Projects Fail: Implementation Challenges in Professional Services*. MIT SMR Research Report.

[5] Grand View Research (2025). *Artificial Intelligence Market Size, Share & Industry Report, 2030*. Available at: https://www.grandviewresearch.com/industry-analysis/artificial-intelligence-ai-market

Chapter 4

[1] Deloitte (2025). 'The Path to Sustainable Generative AI Value Balances Passion, Pragmatism and Patience, Finds New Deloitte Survey'. *PR Newswire.* Available at: https://www.prnewswire.com/news-releases/the-path-to-sustainable-generative-ai-value-balances-passion-pragmatism-and-patience-finds-new-deloitte-survey-302355026.html

Chapter 5

[1] McKinsey & Company (2025). 'Superagency in the workplace: Empowering people to unlock AI's full potential at work'. McKinsey Digital. Available at: https://www.mckinsey.com/capabilities/mckinsey-digital/our-insights/superagency-in-the-workplace-empowering-people-to-unlock-ais-full-potential-at-work

[2] Writer (2025). *Enterprise AI Adoption Report.* Writer Research.

[3] Fortune (2025). 'This CEO laid off nearly 80% of his staff because they refused to adopt AI fast enough. 2 years later, he says he'd do it again'. Available at: https://fortune.com/2025/01/14/ceo-laid-off-80-percent-workforce-ai-sabotage/

[4] McKinsey & Company (2025). 'Superagency in the workplace: Empowering people to unlock AI's full potential at work'. McKinsey Digital. Available at: https://www.mckinsey.com/capabilities/mckinsey-digital/our-insights/superagency-in-the-workplace-empowering-people-to-unlock-ais-full-potential-at-work

[5] Schmidt, E., Rosenberg, J. and Eagle, A. (2019). *Trillion Dollar Coach: The Leadership Playbook of Silicon Valley's Bill Campbell.* New York: Harper Business.

[6] Fortune (2025). 'This CEO laid off nearly 80% of his staff because they refused to adopt AI fast enough. 2 years later, he says he'd do it again'. Available at: https://fortune.com/2025/01/14/ceo-laid-off-80-percent-workforce-ai-sabotage/

[7] Edmondson, A.C. (2018). *The Fearless Organization: Creating Psychological Safety in the Workplace for Learning, Innovation, and Growth.* New York: John Wiley & Sons.

[8] World Economic Forum (2024). 'From Sam Altman to António Guterres: Here's what 10 leaders said about AI at Davos 2024'. Available at: https://www.weforum.org/stories/2024/01/what-leaders-said-about-ai-at-davos-2024/

Chapter 6

[1] PwC (2025). *PwC's AI Agent Survey*. Available at: https://www.pwc.com/us/en/tech-effect/ai-analytics/ai-agent-survey.html

[2] MIT Sloan Management Review (2024). *AI Implementation Challenges in Executive Decision-Making*. MIT SMR Research Report, Q3 2024.

[3] OpenAI (2024). 'Morgan Stanley uses AI evals to shape the future of financial services'. OpenAI Case Studies. Available at: https://openai.com/index/morgan-stanley/

Epilogue

[1] Deloitte (2024). *Future of Work in the Age of AI: Executive Survey Results. Deloitte Insights*. Available at: https://www2.deloitte.com/global/en/insights/focus/technology-and-the-future-of-work.html

[2] Nadella, S. (2024). *AI and the Future of Work*. Microsoft Build 2024 Keynote, Seattle, WA.

[3] Gates, B. (2023). 'The Age of AI has begun'. *Gates Notes*. Available at: https://www.gatesnotes.com/The-Age-of-AI-Has-Begun

[4] Benioff, M. (2024). *Keynote Address*. Dreamforce 2024. Salesforce, San Francisco, CA.

[5] MacDonald, A. (2015). 'Why should anyone bank with you?' *London Business School Review*, 26(1), 35-39.

[6] Huang, J. (2024). *AI's Potential and Responsibility*. NVIDIA GTC 2024 Keynote, San Jose, CA.

[7] Porter, M.E. (1996). 'What is Strategy?' *Harvard Business Review*, November-December 1996.

[8] Grove, A.S. (1996). *Only the Paranoid Survive: How to Exploit the Crisis Points That Challenge Every Company*. New York: Currency Doubleday.

INDEX

visit bionicadvisor.ai

Activate your three trust multipliers.

"This readiness assessment helps you blend human judgement with AI leverage across the three trust multipliers"

www.ingramcontent.com/pod-product-compliance
Lightning Source LLC
LaVergne TN
LVHW011519200926
848484LV00001B/71
* 9 7 8 1 7 6 4 3 3 4 2 0 4 *